BRITAIN'S
LIVING
SEAS

BRITAIN'S LIVING SEAS

Our Coastal Wildlife and How We Can Save It

HANNAH RUDD

BLOOMSBURY WILDLIFE

LONDON · OXFORD · NEW YORK · NEW DELHI · SYDNEY

The Wildlife Trusts

The Wildlife Trusts are a grassroots movement of people from a wide range of backgrounds and all walks of life who share a set of common beliefs. We believe the natural world is valuable in its own right and is the foundation of our wellbeing and prosperity. Everyone deserves to live in a healthy, wildlife-rich natural world.

BLOOMSBURY WILDLIFE
Bloomsbury Publishing Plc
50 Bedford Square, London, WC1B 3DP, UK
29 Earlsfort Terrace, Dublin 2, Ireland

BLOOMSBURY, BLOOMSBURY WILDLIFE and the Diana logo are trademarks of Bloomsbury Publishing Plc

First published in the United Kingdom 2023

A catalogue record for this book is available from the British Library

Library of Congress Cataloguing-in-Publication data has been applied for

ISBN: 978-1-4729-8849-2;
ePub: 978-1-4729-8842-3;
ePDF: 978-1-4729-8841-6

10 9 8 7 6 5 4 3 2 1

Designed by Austin Taylor
Printed and bound in India by Replika Press Pvt. Ltd.

MIX
Paper from responsible sources
FSC® C016779

To find out more about our authors and books visit www.bloomsbury.com and sign up for our newsletters

Contents

Introduction

When we think of the ocean, we may imagine azure blue waters brimming with tropical fish in a gorgeous far-flung location where palm trees line a sandy beach. If you've watched any ocean documentaries, the filmmakers were probably focussed on magical-looking coral reefs or familiar charismatic species like sea turtles and dolphins. But the seas around the British Isles have so much to offer us right on our front doorstep. You don't need to go to the other side of the world to witness enormous whales, swim with sharks or spot playful seals. We often overlook life below our waves, yet our seas are bustling with activity and are no less exciting than those found further afield. British waters may be colder to explore than waters off other shores, yet our spectacular kelp forests and intricate rocky reefs, mud plains and offshore open ocean are home to an abundance of mesmerising creatures that deserve our attention.

Although we geographically split Earth's bodies of water into five oceans and fifty seas, they connect as one enormous entity. This global ocean unites us all. It is vital to our existence and provides humanity with a variety of lifegiving services. Did you know that plankton in our ocean produce half of all the oxygen we breathe? Or that the ocean itself is an integral part of the global climate system? The ocean provides food for at least three billion people across the planet, and the emerging blue economy is supporting millions of diverse livelihoods in coastal communities. And those are just a few of the incredible ways the ocean influences our daily lives.

There's no excuse not to let at least a little bit of the ocean into our lives. Historically, the waters around the British Isles have played a leading role in key events and our overall development as countries. As maritime nations, the sea holds great cultural significance to us, and we should feel strongly about how we manage the waters around the British Isles. The future of our seas and how we choose to use them can hugely impact the people who have come to depend upon them. Around the British Isles, coastal communities are supported primarily by commercial fisheries and the coastal tourism and recreation sectors. But the plummeting condition of our seas is hanging their collective future in the balance.

We have taken our seas for granted for too long, and now they are suffocating because of our actions. The very ecological diversity that makes them so unique also makes them so vulnerable to exploitation. We are fishing our seas unsustainably, polluting them with harmful chemicals and problematic plastics, and dredging precious habitats searching for building materials. Our waters face an even bleaker future as our climate continues to warm and becomes more acidic and too hot to sustain much of its fragile biodiversity. To understand how we can achieve a sustainable future here on Earth, we must also address how we reached this point.

We are at a pivotal moment in our planet's history. If we choose to, we can all make tangible differences in our daily lives to improve the prospects for our ocean and its marine life. Given a chance nature can come back from the darkest of circumstances. We can all be marine conservationists. Establishing a connection with our marine biodiversity is the first step toward conserving it. We are more likely to protect what we love and understand. And you don't need a degree in marine biology or to spend your days in coastal habitats. Every one of us can choose to change our ocean's future.

Throughout this book, I will take you on a journey through our nation's waters and introduce you to many of the marvels that live beneath our waves. I'll demonstrate to you how vital our ocean is to all of us and show how it is suffering enormously due to our everyday actions. We can turn the tide if we follow a roadmap to sustainable seas. As you will see, there is already plenty of oceanic optimism around. Anyone can become a protector of the big blue by implementing simple swaps and connecting with our breathtaking coastline and the organisms that call it home. Together, we can make a positive difference to the future of our marine ecosystems. This book will demonstrate how even the most modest changes benefit our sea-dwelling friends, so let's get started.

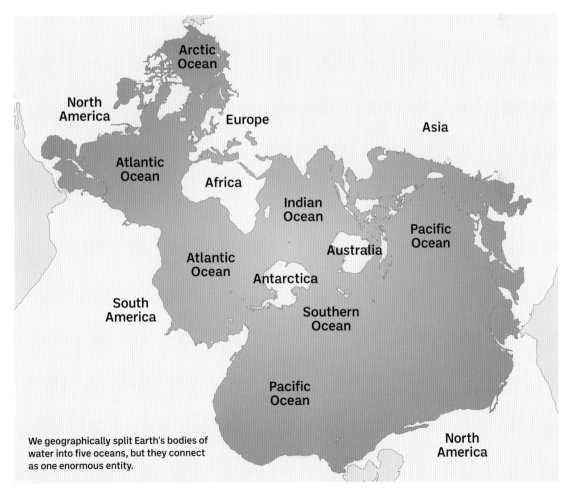

We geographically split Earth's bodies of water into five oceans, but they connect as one enormous entity.

CHAPTER 1

Our Living Seas

What comes to mind when you think of the coastlines around the British Isles? Many think of shingle beaches, rocky outcrops, and a muddy seabed with murky waters devoid of life. Because of this misconception, our coast is often overlooked and undervalued. Yet if you take a closer look, you will find there's much more than first meets the eye.

In the UK, we are blessed to have one of the most exciting coastlines in the world. Our marine environment is brimming with life, with inspiring dynamic headlands, expansive sandy beaches, magical kelp forests and enchanted reefs. All these ecosystems are dynamic environments, ever-changing with the currents, prevailing winds and available nutrients, alongside other environmental influences and human pressures. In this chapter, we will dive into the array of coastal and marine environments that we have in the UK and shine a light on some of the wonderful wildlife you can find inhabiting them.

Magnificent Maritime Cliffs

Dramatic cliff faces are synonymous with our coastline. From the rugged Jurassic Coast in southern England to the wave-battered cliffs of St. Kilda's in the Scottish Outer Hebrides, the UK possesses many internationally important wildlife sites within its maritime cliffs. These landscapes also hold historical and cultural significance to our nation, with coastal icons such as the White Cliffs of Dover (below) symbolising home to many British people.

Maritime cliffs are continually changing as erosional forces like wave action and strong winds chip away at their substrate. As a result, cliff stability varies depending on the type of rock the cliffs comprise and the intensity of eroding forces. Typically, they can be broadly

distinguished as either hard cliffs or soft cliffs.

Hard cliffs are usually steep rock faces 300m high or more, and are composed of hard rocks such as granite, limestone or basalt. They are the most widely distributed form of maritime cliff here in the UK, and they are particularly prevalent along the south coast of England. Hard cliffs are crucial habitats for the numerous internationally significant seabird populations that breed and feed along our coastline. Skomer Island (right), for example, is a haven for puffins that migrate there annually to breed. You can see guillemots, razorbills and kittiwakes nesting on bare ledges, whereas gulls and fulmars are typically more scattered. If you identify a large, untidy nest, it probably belongs to a cormorant or shag – two species that are strikingly similar in appearance.

Hard cliffs are harsh environments. A cliff face offers very limited opportunity for plants to successfully colonise the environment, with often only a hard substrate available and ongoing environmental pressures like salt spray and oncoming tidal surges during storms. Only the sturdiest of plants survive here. Toward the water's edge on the lower cliff faces, you may observe salt-tolerant species like lichens and rock samphire, whereas on the top of the cliff you are likely to see a more varied community of plants within the maritime grassland, such as sea carrot or heath.

With their sheer drops, navigating these steep cliff faces is usually quite challenging, so be careful if you venture to the coast searching for seabirds. It is far safer to bring a pair of binoculars and scan the skyline for the dramatic aerial displays played out by these impressive birds. Hard cliffs may be challenging to explore, but they are well worth it for the sights and sounds you can experience.

Soft cliffs vary in composition and height and are more limited in distribution. You can find great examples of soft maritime cliffs in Cardigan Bay in Wales and the Isle of Skye off the Scottish coast. Soft cliffs allow the colonisation of significantly more life, often featuring diverse communities of grassland, scrub and marsh that thrive on the soft, nutrient-filled substrate. Soft cliffs are vital to invertebrates as they can seek refuge by burrowing into their surface for shelter or undergoing fundamental life stages. Mining bees, solitary wasps and tiger beetles all thrive here. In fact, in the UK, there are 29 invertebrate species that only live in soft-cliff environments. Sand martins are also a species to watch for. These unique birds flit back and forth from their burrows in the soft cliffsides in search of food and nesting materials.

GANNET

Morus bassanus

Streamlined torpedoes, above and below the waves, gannets are a sight to behold – especially when diving from heights of 30m into a bait ball, hitting the water at speeds of up to 60mph. Gannets are meticulously designed by evolution to survive this immense impact, with an extensive network of air-sacs between their muscles and skin to soften the force. They are easily recognisable; very large with mostly white plumage and iconic blue-ringed eyes. It's believed that there are 220,000 pairs of gannets nesting around our coastline – approximately 60–70 percent of the global population. Coastal cliffs on Scottish islands and in locations around Wales and north-east England are hotspots for gannets, with Bass Rock in Scotland holding a

world-famous nesting colony. One thing is for sure, before you see them, you will definitely hear them, and smell them. Large seabird colonies tend to have a unique scent comprised of guano, fresh salty air, and the remnants of leftover fish.

RAZORBILL

Alca torda

Razorbills are medium-sized auks that hunt fish by diving from the surface and swimming underwater. These black and white birds look very similar to penguins, though are not related to them, being stout and upright with black-and-white plumage. They are often seen on the lower ledges of cliff faces and deep ravines, where you may also notice other seabirds like guillemots and puffins in spring and summer as they come to shore to breed. Razorbills can look for prey more than 50m below the surface, and remarkably they've even been spotted by submersibles –an incredible feat for a seabird! The best time to see razorbills is around cliffs from March to July, especially along the Scottish coast and northern England.

PUFFIN

Fratercula arctica

Perhaps one of the most beloved seabird gracing our coastline, the puffin is a charming species to encounter. With its bright orange bill and tuxedoed appearance, it is one of the most remarkable looking seabird species in the world. Puffins spend the harsh winter at sea before returning in their thousands to UK shores in the spring to nest in hobbit-like burrows in the ground. They breed in spring and summer in colonies at key sites in England, Scotland,

Wales and Northern Ireland, such as the Isle of May in the Firth of Forth, and Skomer island off Pembrokeshire, which provide spectacular sightings year upon year. During courtship rituals, male puffins use their vibrant bills to attract a mate as females consider the male with the brightest bill to be the most handsome. Puffins are mostly monogamous and mate for life. Puffin chicks have arguably the most adorable name in the animal kingdom– pufflings – and they keep their parents continually busy fishing for sand eels to build their strength. Interestingly, researchers have recently unveiled that puffin bills glow under ultraviolet light. Whilst scientists don't fully understand why puffins have this unique adaption, they think it may be for breeding purposes.

GUILLEMOT
Uria aalge

Guillemots, like razorbills and puffins, are auks and reside on coastal cliff faces where they nest together, using narrow ledges to keep them safe from predators. They have the smallest nesting territory of any UK bird species, with only around a beak's length between their nest and the next. Their eggs are very tapered in comparison to those of other seabird species. This unique shape is thought to make the egg more stable, balancing on the perilous cliff ledge within its nest, rather than rolling off into the sea below. At a mere three weeks old, guillemot chicks jump off the cliff into the sea – they're pretty hardcore, even from an early age. The adult is a chocolate-brown and white bird that develops a white face during the winter months. Guillemots can be

seen nesting on many coastal cliffs across the UK coastline but are most prevalent in the north of England and in Scotland. During the winter months they spend most of their time offshore, so encountering one is less likely at this time of year.

Special Saltmarsh and Miraculous Mudflats

Vast expanses of mudflats and saltmarsh surround many of the UK's estuaries and natural harbours, particularly around inland tidal areas like the Thames Estuary, and Welwick Saltmarsh on the banks of the River Humber. Mudflats and saltmarshes are a haven for wildlife – especially for wading birds, which relish the opportunity to probe down into the mud with their bills to forage for invertebrates like bristle worms and mud snails.

(continued overleaf)

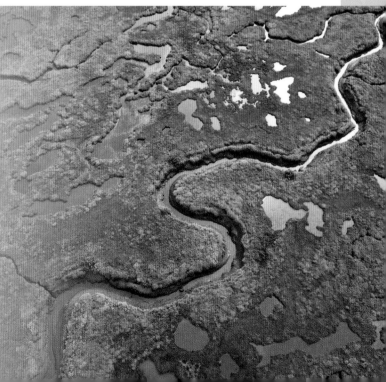

Mudflats are nutrient-rich areas of sheltered estuaries and natural harbours, formed by fine silt and clay sediments settling. They have a high concentration of organic material and are plentiful food sources, making them the perfect place to find invertebrates.

Saltmarsh, on the other hand, is created when saltwater floods marshland before retreating again to the sea, leaving a nutrient-rich mud behind for vegetation like sea aster, cord-grasses and sea purslane to colonise. Saltmarsh is also a nature-based solution to the climate crisis. You can read more about its astonishing carbon-absorbing properties later.

CURLEW
Numenius arquata

Curlews are large wading birds that are a frequent sight along saltmarsh and mudflats throughout the country, especially in autumn and winter, foraging for worms, bivalves and cockles. They make a distinctive call during the breeding months of February through to July, which sounds like 'cur-lee'. Curlews can be observed around the UK coastline, especially in and around large, undisturbed estuarine areas. Morecambe Bay, the Wash, the Humber Estuary and the Severn Estuary have the largest curlew populations that you can encounter off our coast.

REDSHANK
Tringa totanus

Redshanks get their name from their characteristic long, bright red legs; the long bill also has a red base. Using their beak like a probe, they rummage around the mudflats for their favourite foods of marine invertebrates, molluscs and crustaceans. Many redshanks migrate to the UK from Iceland to overwinter along our coastline. They can be spotted throughout a range of habitats, especially in Scotland and northern England, on saltmarshes, mudflats and marshes.

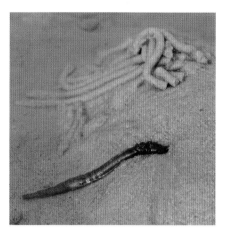

LUGWORM
Arenicola marina

Have you ever noticed those small squiggles of sand on beaches? They are known as casts and are an indicator of a lugworm burrow. They are found on mudflats and sandy beaches, and are formed by lugworms ingesting the substrate and then pooping it out to create a similar shape to themselves along the shoreline. Lugworms are either bright red or a mottled brown in colour and feed on detritus that they filter from the sand as they make their burrows. You can find their casts all along our shores, but lugworms are rarely seen, other than by fishers who dig them for bait. They are also a favourite snack for many wading birds.

OYSTERCATCHER
Haematopus ostralegus

With its loud call and distinguished look, the oystercatcher is a familiar sight (and sound) of the coast. Its defining features are an elongated orange bill, pinky-red legs, and a predominantly black head, back and wings with a white underbelly. It also has piercing red eyes that contrast beautifully against its black head. Its long and flattened bill is well adapted for forcing open its favourite shellfish species – cockles and muscles. Oystercatchers have a widespread distribution around the UK coastline but over the last 50 years they have begun to move further inland to breed on waterways and lakes. During the wintertime most UK resident oystercatchers are found around the coast at large estuaries, where migrants accompany them from Norway and Iceland. They will forage on both rocky and sandy coastlines, and form large roosts at high tide.

Sleek Sand Dunes

Sand dunes are spectacular ecosystems that are continually in motion. Shaped by the power of Mother Nature, these uniquely delicate yet vast entities allow an abundance of wildlife to thrive. They are distributed widely around our coastline, but the Hebrides in Scotland and the south coast of England are hotspots and are home to larger sand dunes. Dunes are typically created in parallel to the beach, becoming progressively taller the further they are from the shoreline. They range from a few to hundreds of years old, with the oldest dune systems located between Liverpool and Southport on the Sefton Coast.

(continued overleaf)

Sand dune systems are facing a precarious future, however, as they become cornered by human developments and farmlands.

Wonderful plants exist within sand dune ecosystems, surprising as this may seem, as their substrate is so dynamic. Wander around fixed dunes in the summer and you will come across clovers, lady's bedstraw, pyramidal orchid, kidney vetch and carline thistle dotted around the place. The best place to look for these and other dune-loving plants are dune systems comprised of lime-rich shell sand as these promote the widest range of plant species. Prickly saltwort, sea rocket, oraches or sea sandwort growing along the strandline are good indicators of a healthy sand dune system.

But it's not only plant diversity that sand dunes promote. They are also home to a variety of invertebrate and reptile species, especially when they warm up in the summer. Keep your eyes open for little piles of sand left behind by burrowing bees and digger wasps as they burrow into the sand. It's also worth looking out for trails left behind by lizards as they move across looser sand.

MARRAM GRASS
Ammophila arenaria

A quintessential plant within a sand dune ecosystem, marram grass stabilises sand dunes by establishing its elongated matted root system. As the marram grass becomes more widespread, it allows other species to colonise the sand dunes as the environment becomes more stable and appealing to life. As a pioneer species, marram grass is well adapted to adversity at the coast. It has glossy, rolled-up leaves that minimise water loss, and its extensive root system draws moisture and nutrients from the surrounding substrate. Flowering in July and August with densely packed golden flowers, marram grass is widespread along the UK coastline where sand dunes are present.

LADY'S BEDSTRAW
Galium verum

With its sweet, honey-like scent and stunning yellow petals, lady's bedstraw is a wonderful assault on the senses during a summer coastal walk. Your best chance of seeing this delicate flower is from June to September when it carpets sand dunes. Lady's bedstraw gets its name from being used historically to stuff the mattresses of women about to give birth.

SAND LIZARD
Lacerta agilis

The sand lizard is one of the rarest and most elusive of the UK's six native reptile species. These relatively small lizards can be found in undulating dunes along our coastline, and hibernate between November and March, emerging in spring ready to mate. Males take on a bright green colour during this time to attract females. Sand lizards are facing an increasingly difficult time as their preferred dune habitat is lost to coastal development. Spotting one of these unique animals is therefore becoming harder. On a warm summer's day, if you look closely at the sand, you may encounter one basking in the sun. Sand dune ecosystems within Dorset, Hampshire, Surrey and Merseyside offer your best chance. Thankfully there are also reintroduction programmes in the south of England, Lancashire and Wales currently taking place to extend their range.

NATTERJACK TOAD
Epidalea calamita

Natterjack toads are one of the UK's rarest amphibians and are found at a small number of locations in Scotland and England. The prefer to inhabit shallow pools on sand dune ecosystems, where they breed. During the springtime they become more active, with the males producing a chorus of 'song' to attract a mate. This call can be heard up to a mile away. They are nocturnal creatures so you will rarely encounter them during the day.

Beautiful Beaches
and Spectacular Strandlines

Beautiful beaches that stretch as far as the eye can see are synonymous with summer holidays. Whether sand or shingle, beaches comprise roughly one-third of the UK coastline and many of us will have fond memories associated with spending family days at the seaside. They are important geologically too, as longshore drift transports sediments along the coast via changing tides and currents, washing them up further along the shoreline to form beaches and spits. It may seem that not a lot is going on in terms of flora and fauna on a beach, other than the odd gull nicking tourists' chips, but our beaches and strandlines are bustling with life.

It may surprise you, but the vegetation along some of the UK's shingle beaches is of global significance. At the strandline, an area formed by the deposition of flotsam and jetsam along the shoreline that is higher than the water level, you can find an array of plants such as prickly saltwort, sea rocket and sea sandwort, which form a row of vegetation. Higher up on shingle beaches you find larger plants. These deep-rooted perennial plants – that is, those that are long-living – are visually appealing and many have intriguing names. Yellow-horned poppy, sea kale, sea mayweed and sea campion all jostle for space above the high tide line. Further up the beach is where you might find more stable plants and trees similar to those in lichen-rich grassland and heathland. Perhaps surprisingly, scrub – a plant community dominated by shrubs – and even woodland can become established on more solid shingle.

Beaches and strandlines provide a home for a range of small invertebrates, including sandhoppers, cockles and lugworms. Micro-habitats are created by waves, which carry material like driftwood to the beach. Sadly, the tides also bring discarded plastics, which can plague our beaches and suffocate marine life – more on this later.

GOOSE BARNACLE

Lepas anatifera

A captivating species, the goose barnacle encapsulates the weird and wonderful of the crustacean world. In fact, it was once believed that these animals were the source of young barnacle geese. They are related to the smaller, rock-encrusting acorn barnacle, and more distantly to crabs and lobsters. They are filter-feeders that have evolved to use their specially adapted legs to capture plankton and detritus as it moves past them through the water. They attach themselves to an eclectic range of objects from rocks to ropes, plastic bottles and driftwood, where they grow in large clumps. They have a delicate chalky-white shell with a long fleshy stem resembling the black neck of the barnacle goose, hence their name.

Goose barnacles are rare on UK shores, but are occasionally washed up in large numbers, attached to flotsam and jetsam after storms along the west and south-west coasts of the UK.

COMMON SEAL

Phoca vitulina

You may know these as 'harbour seals', but they are also widely known as common seals. This is a confusing name for them, as they are not as common as the other seal species in the UK, the grey seal. When common seals aren't out at sea hunting for their favourite diet of fish, squid, whelks and crab, these adorable animals are hauled out on sandbanks and beaches that line sheltered shores and estuaries. You may be lucky enough to see them in their signature curved banana position. Their most important haul-out locations are in the Hebrides, Orkney and the Shetland Islands, as well as along the Wash in the east of England. Common seals can be told from grey seals by their more finely speckled coats, their small-headed proportions, a concave head profile with a short, dog-like snout, and their nostrils, which are less vertical than those of the grey seal.

RINGED PLOVER
Charadrius hiaticula

Following the rhythm of the rain, ringed plovers are charming little birds that tap their feet on the ground to lure their underground-dwelling prey out from their burrows. This fascinating behaviour is known as 'foot-trembling'. The ringed plover is a common resident around the UK coast and is even observed around flooded gravel pits and reservoirs. Ringed plovers from Europe spend their winters in Britain, whereas those from Greenland and Canada stopover during their migration. The species is a little larger than the little ringed plover and lacks a yellow ring around its eye. Its plumage changes slightly with the seasons, but its orange and black stumpy bill remains one of its most striking features year-round.

TURNSTONE
Arenaria interpres

Named after their habit of turning over large stones, turnstones can be seen all year, despite not breeding here in the UK. Turnstones from northern Europe migrate here in the summer months and leave again in the spring, whereas those from Canada and Greenland arrive in early autumn and leave in early summer, providing us with a year-round presence. They are medium-sized waders that have a varied diet. Their plumage changes in colouration with the season. During the summer months they have a chestnut and black chequered plumage, whereas during the winter months they lose this pattern and are instead dark brown with a black face and breast and a white underbelly.

Bountiful Biogenic Reefs

Biogenic reefs provide a complex array of habitats for marine life, typically in the UK made by blue or horse mussels, honeycomb worms or ross tubeworms, or native oysters, often growing to several metres in height and diameter. They form a crucial ecosystem supporting life in our seas, and were once plentiful across temperate marine regions. The foundations of mussel biogenic reefs are naturally created by the mussels binding dead and living shells together using sand and mud. Honeycomb and Ross worms also build reefs, using tubes of sand. If you're lucky enough to encounter a biogenic reef, you will usually find it submerged within the subtidal zone – the area that is never exposed to air. Here the reef-building species have continual access to new deposits of sand as the current brings in new material for expanding the reefs' structure. Biogenic reefs are rare as only a limited number of species can create them. Their distribution throughout the UK is rather restricted, with the most northerly limit of the Outer Hebrides and the south-west coast of England being considered hotspots.

EUROPEAN FLAT OYSTER

Ostrea edulis

Once abundant around the British coastline, native oysters have experienced a steep decline thanks to our love of their taste. Oysters are bivalve molluscs, which means they have two shells. In their case, however, their two shells are not identical: one is round, and the other is flat like a lid. They inhabit the seabed in shallow coastal waters and estuaries, and when conditions are favourable, they will form dense oyster beds. These hard-shelled creatures are wonderful filter-feeders, filtering plankton and detritus from the surrounding water column (the column of water that extends downwards from the surface to the substrate on the bottom).

Nearly all oysters start life as males but can change sex regularly throughout their lives, depending on the surrounding water temperature. Contrary to common belief, native oysters don't produce commercially viable pearls.

HONEYCOMB WORM

Sabellaria alveolata

Named after the honeycomb-like reef structure it builds (see photo), the honeycomb worm is another core biogenic reef-building species. It creates a protective tube around itself comprising sand and shell fragments from the seafloor. These filter-feeders then extend their feeding tentacles into the surrounding water column to entrap floating plankton or marine detritus as it floats past. With their numerous nooks and crannies, honeycomb reefs provide habitats and shelter for many other species. It's estimated that a well-established reef can support roughly 38 different species. For the honeycomb worm to be able to construct its tube home, it requires a hard substrate to act as a foundation. For this reason, there are only a handful of places in the UK where the balance between foundations and building materials is just right. The southern and western coastlines of Britain and Northern Ireland provide hotspots, with very few records in eastern regions.

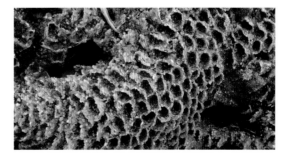

ROSS WORM
Sabellaria spinulosa

Ross worms are small polychaete, or 'bristle' worms (a class of segmented worm, found mostly within the marine environment, with protrusions that resemble bristles), typically found subtidally but occasionally found very low in the intertidal zone – where the shoreline is submerged during high tide and exposed during low tide. They can only build biogenic reefs in favourable conditions, but when these are met their reefs can extend over several hectares and be approximately 60cm high, so they are an impressive feat of biological engineering. These conditions are only present in a handful of locations across the UK, so seeing a Ross worm reef is rare. It is possible though to observe them in smaller communities that encrust kelp holdfasts and bedrock. The worms construct their tubes out of sand and shell fragments that they collect from the drifting current.

BLUE MUSSEL
Mytilus edulis

Mussels are perhaps one of the most well-recognised bivalves thanks to our appetite for them, but they are also a common sight around the UK coastline and are a staple food for many marine species. They are quite adaptable and can be found in a variety of marine habitats including rocky reefs, sandy bottoms or muddy estuaries. If undisturbed, mussels aggregate together to form vast and dense mussel beds that can cover the seabed. Using sticky fibres known as byssus threads, they attach themselves to the seabed to ensure they don't drift away with strong currents or tidal surges. Their incredible water purification abilities are like those of oysters. They suck in enormous volumes of seawater whilst feeding on plankton, and during this process clean the water.

Rockin' Rocky Reefs

Rocky reefs count for a large area of our coastline, and remind many people who grew up in the UK of childhoods spent clambering around them. Thanks to the varied nature of rocky reefs, there are many different types of these fascinating habitats, perfect for attracting a wide diversity of life to their nooks and crannies. Rocky reefs are also either permanently or periodically submerged beneath the water, so they are constantly changing.

There are distinct zones within a rocky shore ecosystem. Within the intertidal zone they offer sanctuary to the wildlife living in this stressful environment. The upper shore is underwater for less time than any other region, so it is home to the most robust creatures. You will probably be the most familiar with this area as it's where you can find limpets, barnacles and sea snails clinging onto the rock faces.

Further toward the surf line, you will encounter more and more seaweed as the environment becomes more tolerable and marine life experiences more interaction with the tide. Seaweeds like bladderwrack can blanket rock faces and the beach, providing a damp shelter for mini marine life like shore crabs and dog whelks. You may also find blennies and other small fish hanging out in small rockpools. As you approach the lower shore waterline, you will begin to observe an increasing abundance of life as the environmental conditions begin to stabilise.

It is in the subtidal zone that you find the most stable communities. Species here do not experience the harsh conditions that affect species in the intertidal zone. Life is smoother and without much disruption. Here, many fish species and extensive algal and animal communities rely upon the rocky reef for survival.

Rocky reefs are one of the most quintessential ecosystems to visit when taking a trip to the UK coastline. Like many other marine environments, they constantly change under dynamic geological and ecological forces. Species are continually competing with one another for precious space and limited resources. Relentless wave action erodes the rocky substrate, creating more crevasses and cracks for marine life to colonise and call home.

STAR ASCIDIAN
Botryllus schlosseri

A spectacular sight, reminiscent of a collection of colourful small flowers, the star ascidian is not one animal but a colony of 3–12 creatures living together, creating a star-shaped pattern. These incredible creatures can be found attached to the underside of rocks or clinging to kelp fronds swaying in the current across the UK along rocky shores, so your chances of spotting one are high. Using a siphon-shaped appendage, they suck up tiny plankton from the surrounding waters.

BEADLET ANEMONE
Actinia equina

The beadlet anemone is commonly found throughout rocky reefs around the UK. It has a vivid red colouration and dainty tentacles that flow with the current. When the tide is in, these animals use their tentacles to sting passing prey like small fish and shrimp, and when it goes out they retract their tentacles inside their bodies. Beadlet anemones may look like stationary organisms, but are highly territorial and engage in duels with other anemones. They defend their favourite spot on the rock using a beautiful bright blue ring of beads underneath their tentacles called acrorrhagi, which are filled with stinging cells.

ORANGE-CLUBBED SEA SLUG
Limacia clavigera

These beautiful nudibranchs (sea slugs) are often spotted grazing on seaweeds along the rocky shore from just below the watermark to at least 20m deep. They are feeding on bryozoans – a colony of animals that live attached to the surface of seaweeds. The orange-clubbed sea slug gets its name from the orange clubs covering its body, which have various different functions, including taste and smell. Some even contain defensive glands, which produce chemicals that taste nasty to other predators and act as a mechanism to stop the sea slug from being eaten. You can spot the orange-clubbed sea slug on all UK coasts, except in extreme south-east England.

CORKWING WRASSE
Symphodus melops

With its gorgeous turquoise-blue pattern, the corkwing wrasse is one of the most iconic rocky reef fish species found in the UK. On a diving adventure you may spot the males building complex nests out of seaweed in shallow water among the rocky crevices from spring into early summer. As with many species, males have the most vibrant colouration with a mixture of blues, greens, oranges and pinks adorning their skin, whereas females are a duller brown. You can distinguish the corkwing wrasse from other wrasse species by the dark spots in the middle of their tails.

CUCKOO WRASSE
Labrus mixtus

At first sight, you might think these stunning fish live in more tropical climates than the UK but you'd be mistaken. The cuckoo wrasse is undeniably one of the most colourful fish that inhabits our seas, and it's a joy to encounter whilst diving or snorkelling around our coastline. Cuckoo wrasse are 'protogynous hermaphrodites', meaning they start life as females but each individual can change sex to become a male when there is a need in the population. This need is usually when the single dominant male on the reef dies, and the most senior female will change sex to become the top male.

COMMON CUTTLEFISH
Sepia officinalis

These curious creatures look like they're from another world. Cuttlefish are related to squids and octopuses, belonging to a group of molluscs known as 'cephalopods', organisms composed of a conjoined head and foot as the name suggests, and characterised by a number of arms or tentacles surrounding the head. They have diverse colours and patterns and can easily mimic their surroundings. Common cuttlefish are fascinating and fierce predators, feasting on crustaceans and small fish. Cuttlefish egg clutches are known as 'sea grapes' due to their black appearance. You may recognise this animal's chalky internal shell, known as 'cuttlebone', from a trip to the beach (or the pet shop).

Striking Seagrass

Seagrass meadows (see top of page 26) are luscious underwater fields and are key weapons in our fight against climate change. Seagrasses are an important coastal defence, preventing coastal erosion as their roots anchor deeply within the substrate, stabilising the seabed. They form a beautiful green carpet that contrasts with the surrounding blue waters.

Seagrasses have the unique attribute of being the only flowering plants that tolerate living in seawater, and here in the UK we have four species, which are found all around our coastline in sheltered habitats like lagoons and bays. Like many plants, seagrasses are dependent on sunlight to photosynthesise and create food to grow. As a result, they can only grow within shallow waters to a depth of approximately 4m. Seagrass meadows are havens for marine life and form critical breeding and nursery grounds for many noteworthy species in the UK.

SHORT-SNOUTED SEAHORSE
Hippocampus hippocampus

One of only two seahorse species in the UK, the short-snouted seahorse is special. It lives in shallow waters, often in estuaries or areas with seagrass meadows, and as it is relatively poor swimmers, its tail grasps seagrass or seaweed to keep it steady in the harsh currents. Short-snouted seahorses don't have teeth. Instead, they suck up their favourite prey of small shrimp and plankton. Seahorses and pipefish are the only animals that we know of that experience a reversed pregnancy. Females transfer their eggs to the males who self-fertilise them, keeping them in their pouches until they're ready to be birthed into the ocean. You can find these enchanting animals from the Shetland Isles down the west coast of the UK and along the south-east coast of England.

BARREL JELLYFISH
Rhizostoma pulmo

As the UK's largest jellyfish, these beautiful creatures are undoubtedly impressive, weighing up to 35kg. It's common to sight them off the southern and western coasts of Britain during the summer, and you may also encounter them washed up on the beaches between May and June – sometimes in their hundreds! These giant jellyfish ingest passing plankton using the hundreds of little mouths on their eight arms, which surround the tiny stinging tentacles called nematocysts. Even though their sting is not life-threatening to humans, it's best not to get too close to these alien-like creatures.

COMMON OCTOPUS
Octopus vulgaris

Easily one of the most intelligent invertebrates in the sea, the common octopus is a master of camouflage and a skilled hunter, with eight long arms and two rows of suckers alongside a secret weapon of venomous glands to incapacitate prey. A nocturnal species, it is mostly observed on the UK's south and west coasts, where it often hides in rocky crevices during the day. Female common octopuses are extremely devoted and spend every moment tending to their eggs until they hatch. Unfortunately the mother usually then dies, due to exhaustion.

EDIBLE CRAB
Cancer pagurus

Common all around UK shores, the edible crab derives its name from being the most consumed crab species in Europe. You may also know this species as the brown crab, so-called because of its colouration. This abundant species lives in the lower inshore areas, but it can also commonly be found to depths of 100m out in the open sea. You may encounter these crabs while scrambling around a rocky shore and taking a peek under boulders, and if you're lucky, you may catch the crab in the act of predation. Edible crabs are active predators and hunt various species, from mussels and whelks, and even dig for prey, like razor clams and otter shells.

Kelp Kingdom

There are few things more charming than a kelp forest – exploring these underwater forests is like being transported to another world. Kelp is the colloquial term for several species of large brown seaweed that frequent temperate coastlines across the globe, including the UK's. It has ingeniously evolved to suit its environment and the powerful swells that sweep through it by having a branching structure

called a 'holdfast' that roots it to the seabed, and broad fronds that enable it to sway freely with the current. This nifty way of anchoring itself to the substrate also provides a complex network of nooks and crannies that provide shelter for hundreds of animals like worms, crustaceans, sea squirts and small fish. You may even find the eggs of larger fish species, such as the lumpsucker, onto the holdfast.

Kelp forests are among the most productive and diverse ecosystems on the planet. They are hugely important in our planet's carbon cycle and capture an astonishing 75 percent of the net carbon fixed annually in the sea. They are also tremendously important in providing coastal protection and slowing the coastal erosion created by intense wave action. As climate change leads to increasingly dramatic weather, kelp forests are becoming increasingly important.

You can find these immense forests around all the coasts of the UK, with forests developing in areas with a suitably rocky seabed. Home to the highest diversity of kelp species in Europe, 7 out of 14 European species are found in our waters. The kelp species found in a given area varies depending on how exposed that area's coast is to wave action. For example, very exposed coasts have lots of winged kelp, whereas less exposed areas hold tangleweed and cuvie, while sugar kelp dominates sheltered coasts.

GREY SEAL

Halichoerus grypus

Affectionately referred to as the 'dogs of the ocean' by conservationists, seals are alluring animals. The grey seal is the larger of the two UK seal species, and you can experience life below the waves with grey seals in hotspots such as the Farne Islands and Lundy Island. Their scientific name means 'hooked-nose sea pig', and if you look closely, you can see why! Grey seals spend most of their time at sea feeding on fish,

but when they return to land, they haul out on beaches. They are an example of a conservation success story too. In the early twentieth century, their numbers dropped to only 500, but today it is estimated that we have more than 120,000 grey seals here in Britain. That's a whopping 40 percent of the world's population. Their pups are also adorable, adorned with a beautiful white fluffy coat when they're born in the autumn months.

BLACK SEA BREAM

Spondyliosoma cantharus

The presence of black sea bream, also known as 'porgy', is another conservation success here in the UK, with select key breeding sites receiving protection and an increase in numbers observed. They are omnivorous fish, with their diets comprising seaweeds and small invertebrates. Black sea bream are protogynous hermaphrodites, which means they are all born as females and change sex to male once they reach 30cm in length. In spring these fish get ready to mate, with the males changing colour to become darker with vertical white bars and the females indicating that they're ready

to lay their eggs by displaying a long horizontal white bar on their bodies. Males dig a shallow depression in the seabed with gravel and sand on the surrounding edges to provide a crater where the female can lay her eggs. The males then protect the eggs from predators like wrasse and whelks until they hatch. Black sea bream prefer warmer waters, and your best chance of encountering them is on the south and west coasts of the UK.

SMALL-SPOTTED CATSHARK

Scyliorhinus canicula

You might know this little shark as a 'dogfish' or 'lesser-spotted dogfish'. These delightful sharks get their names from the dark spots covering their skin, and they curl up into a doughnut shape when they feel threatened. As the name suggests, the small-spotted catshark is a member of the catshark family and is an oviparous species, laying eggs – commonly known as mermaids' purses – that you may find washed up on beaches around the UK coastline. Catsharks are mesopelagic predators, in that they live in depths between 200m and 1,000m, and feed on small crabs, molluscs and fish. Like all sharks, they have a crucial role in managing marine ecosystems by keeping their prey populations at a healthy level.

Cool Cold-water Corals

Charming coral reefs are not only a feature of distant destinations and tropical archipelagos. They are also located here in the UK, just not in the format you might first think. Instead of being situated in shallow warm waters like their tropical counterparts, the UK's coral reefs are in the dark depths of the temperate sea. Deep-water corals are those that grow in chilly waters that range in temperature from 4°C to 12°C. Also, unlike their shallow-water relatives, deep-water corals do not depend upon a symbiotic relationship with zooxanthellae, a unique species of algae, for their growth or survival. As a result, they grow at an astonishingly slow rate.

WHAT IS BIOLUMINESCENCE?

An iridescent oceanic light show, bioluminescence is one of the many wonders of the natural world. It is an entirely organic process whereby living organisms produce and emit light as a result of chemical reactions taking place within the organism itself. Bioluminescence within the ocean is particularly common in the deep sea (generally below 200m), where natural light cannot penetrate, and is used by organisms for crucial behaviours, from finding a mate to alluring prey or scaring off predators. Sometimes it can also be seen closer to shore – Aberavon Beach in Port Talbot and Grouville in Jersey are considered UK hotspots. It's used by organisms of all sizes, from minuscule bacteria to enormous squids. Scientists still have lots to learn about the intricacies of bioluminescence and its uses within the ocean.

Due to their very nature, it's doubtful you'll ever be able to experience the vast wonders of UK deep-sea corals with your own eyes unless you are a fortunate soul. Within our waters, they are found off the north and west coasts of Scotland and off the western Irish coastline, particularly the Mingulay Reef Complex just 13km off the island of Mingulay in Scotland.

The most remarkable deep-sea coral mounds in the UK are the Darwin Mounds, located 160km north-west of Cape Wrath, Scotland, at the north end of the Rockall Trough. First discovered by researchers from the University of Glasgow in 1998, they comprise two series of coral mounds at a depth of approximately 1,000m, covering a total area of 100km².

LOPHELIA
Lophelia pertusa

Lophelia is the most common coral in our waters. It's an intricate stony coral that feeds on zooplankton, crustaceans and krill carried by the surrounding currents. It is estimated to grow at an average of 10mm a year, compared with approximately 20mm a year for warm-water corals. It's thought that some coral mounds can be a whopping 8,000 years old. And these mounds are not only crucial for corals but also for the abundance of species for which they provide a home; animals like starfish, sponges, anemones, redfish and squat lobster, alongside many commercially important species like cod

and shore crab. They are also vitally important feeding grounds, spawning and nursery sites for these species, offering protection from strong currents and predators.

PINK SEA FAN
Eunicella verrucosa

Pink sea fan is a type of horny coral known as a gorgonian, and is one of the many species in UK seas protected by law. Like all corals, pink sea fans are slow-growing, and despite their name, pink sea fans can also be orange and white. They are a globally significant species and have only a few strongholds remaining in the UK, in south-west England and south Wales, in shallow waters between 10m and 50m deep. Their fan shape provides lots of different nooks and crannies for other smaller creatures to inhabit.

PHOSPHORESCENT SEA PEN

Pennatula phosphorea

Reminiscent of a Harry Potter prop, sea pens are unmistakable creatures. Incredibly, each sea pen is not an individual animal but a colony of mini anemone-like creatures called polyps that live together, each with a specific role. They are filter-feeders, and the colony includes specialised feeding polyps known as autozooids that can capture food particles as they pass in the current. When they are disturbed, phosphorescent sea pens bioluminesce, faintly lighting up the sea with white polyps on their slender pinkish frame. This light display also helps to ward off predators. Sea pens inhabit the deep seabed of the North Sea, Northern Irish Sea and Scottish sea lochs.

DEAD MAN'S FINGERS

Alcyonium digitatum

The name of this species of soft coral originates from its resemblance to the fingers on a human hand. Like all corals, dead man's fingers is a colony of individual small animals – known as polyps – that thrive together by sharing a gelatinous skeleton. With branching tentacles, each polyp protrudes into the surrounding sea to feed on passing plankton. During the autumn months, the polyps prepare for spawning and do not feed at all during this period. Don't confuse them with red fingers, which is an entirely different species with white feeding tentacles and slimmer dark red fingers.

Silky Sand and Gritty Gravel

You might think sand and gravel aren't the most exciting of marine environments. They lack the majesty of a kelp forest, or the awe of a coral reef, so they may initially appear a little dull in comparison. Yet mud, sand and gravel habitats collectively comprise up to 90 percent of our seabed and are vital environments for many species. It's rare to have sand without the gravel. In the North Sea, you will typically find sand and gravel derived from hard rocks, whereas around the west coast and in the English Channel and the Irish Sea they are more likely to be composed of shells. All habitats are connected, so the composition of these habitats varies depending on the nearby coastline.

Sand and gravel environments rely on the ocean's dynamism and power. They are formed through erosion when substrates enter the sea after being worn down from maritime cliffs, rocky reefs and beaches. Over time the substrate particles become smaller and smaller, forming gravel and sand. These particles are then easily carried by the current and are constantly shifting with the movements of the sea.

Because they are so soft and dynamic, sand habitats are particularly popular with burrowing sea creatures like lugworms that enjoy squeezing themselves down into the seabed. Sand and gravel are also vital for supporting some of the most important species in our marine food chains – sand eels. Larger species like plaice and other flatfish camouflage themselves impeccably against the seabed, making it easier to stalk unsuspecting prey and take advantage of an easy meal. Be cautious of the lesser weever fish – this feisty fellow burrows itself in the sand, leaving its eyes and venomous spines exposed to drift in the current, and could leave a nasty injury if trodden on.

On the other hand, gravel is generally formed of larger particles than sand. It is a more stable environment, giving animal and plant communities an easier time colonising the habitat. From anemones to sea cucumbers and sponges to black sea bream, you can find many magical underwater wonders thriving on gravel.

BLONDE RAY

Raja brachyura

Despite its name, the blonde ray isn't a ray at all – it's a skate. This giant skate enjoys spending its time on the sandy bottom where its beige-coloured skin with small dark and pale spots camouflage it against the seafloor from predators lurking above. The English Channel is an important breeding site for blonde rays in the UK, and they usually aggregate in this area between April and July. Being one of the larger species of skate we get here in the UK, the blonde ray's diet is varied and includes bigger animals like cuttlefish alongside the usual favourites of small crustaceans and molluscs.

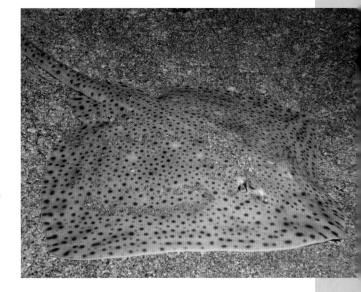

RED GURNARD
Chelidonichthys cuculus

Known affectionately as 'sea robins', gurnards are brightly coloured fish that are easily recognisable thanks to their pectoral fins being reminiscent of legs, making them appear to walk along the seabed. The red gurnard is one of six gurnard species found in the UK and is a bottom-dwelling species found in various habitats including gravel, sand, or rocky seabeds.

PLAICE
Pleuronectes platessa

Look closely at the sandy seabed, and you may catch a glimpse of beady eyes sticking out above the sediment. Brilliantly camouflaged against the substrate with a mottled colouration, the plaice is a diamond-shaped flatfish that can be hard to spot. You can differentiate plaice from other flatfish species thanks to their vibrant orange spots. Remarkably all flatfish begin life looking like typical fish with one eye on each side of their heads. As a plaice one eye begins to migrate to the right side of its head, but it may be the left side in other flatfish species. Plaice can be found all around the UK, with younger fish typically found close to shore and in estuaries.

SAND EELS
Ammodytidae

In many ways, sand eels are the bread and butter of our marine food chains. A vast array of ocean life is dependent on them – they fatten up everything from puffin chicks to migrating mackerel, and they are a favourite snack of harbour porpoises. Surprisingly they are not eels at all. 'Sand eel' is a colloquial term used to describe an array of different small fish species within the sand lance family, with their distinctively slender bodies and pointed snouts that form an eel-like shape. You may see these important fish between April and September when they swim in large shoals close to the seabed around our coast – perhaps you'll catch a glimpse of them burrowing into the sand to evade predators (like you!). In the bleak winter months, they spend all their time buried in sand.

Marvellous Mud

Mud may appear featureless, but believe it or not, it is teeming with marine life. Essentially it is fine silt and clay that is constantly or occasionally covered by water, and like other marine environments, it is continually shifting and changing with the external forces of the ocean. Soft mud supports larger species that often grow faster, whereas sandy mud habitats support many smaller animals. Intertidal mudflats around the UK coastline cover approximately 270,000 hectares, typically sheltered coastal inlets like estuaries and harbours. Wildlife in the deep sea also particularly likes muddy habitats. You can find an abundance of weird and wonderful creatures inhabiting the muddy bottom, from brittlestars to spider crabs and lobsters, with alien-like bristleworms burrowing into the mud.

SCAMPI
Nephrops norvegicus

If you enjoy seafood, you've probably tucked into a meal of scampi and chips. Also known as langoustine, nephrops, Dublin Bay prawns or the Norway lobster, this is one of the most commercially important species throughout Europe. Scampi are nocturnal creatures, choosing to bury themselves in the seabed during the daytime and coming out under cover of night to prey on crustaceans, molluscs, worms and starfish. Scampi are highly territorial and aggressively defend their burrows from intruders, leaving only to mate or feed after dark.

SPINY SPIDER CRAB
Maja brachydactyla

Spiny spider crabs are reminiscent of a creature from a science-fiction movie. They are a large migratory crab species with very long legs and a shell covered in spines. For a crab, their annual 100-mile migration to deeper waters during the autumn months is especially impressive. Sometimes their shells can be covered in green algae, which gives them a hairy look. They're not fussy eaters either and will feed on anything they can get their pincers on, including seaweed, small fish and starfish. Spiny spider crabs are common offshore of south and west England and Wales.

COMMON COCKLE

Cerastoderma edule

Cockles are synonymous with a trip to the seaside, although many of us may be more familiar with them as a treat doused in malt vinegar. These bivalves reside on muddy and sandy shores, where they prefer to spend their time between the intertidal and subtidal zones. Due to their preference for mud, they often occupy estuaries. They have a distinctive shell, adorned with smooth domed ridges and raised rough ridges in a symmetrical pattern. Similar to other bivalves, cockles are filter-feeders and obtain their food from the passing organic matter and plankton. They are also a fundamental element of the marine food web and provide an important source of protein for many wading birds, crustaceans and flatfish.

TOPE

Galeorhinus galeus

Growing up to 2m long, this beautiful shark is a favourite target of recreational anglers and rarely observed by other ocean users, despite being found close to shore along our coastline. Tope can live for more than 50 years and so like other shark species they are very slow growing and late maturing, meaning they are especially vulnerable to human activities.

Tope have an eclectic diet and feed on a wide range of marine life, from smaller fish species to crustaceans and cephalopods. Tagging studies have shown that they regularly travel enormous distances, with some individuals tagged in the UK reaching the Canary Islands and the Azores in the mid-Atlantic. Tope can be found all around the UK coast, but they are more commonly encountered in the south and west. Never fear, there has never been a recorded attack on a human by a tope.

Boundless Pelagic

Many of us will only witness the high seas when we travel to foreign countries and peer out of an aeroplane window thousands of feet up. Yet this area covers almost half of our planet's surface area and provides over 90 percent of its living space. It is the location of enormous and significant migration events, vital feeding grounds and precious breeding sites. The open ocean is split into a number of layers, with the

pelagic – covering the uppermost layers of the open ocean – being the site of much biological activity. It provides a connection between coastal areas too, for species to move from one area to another, like the migration of European eels from the Sargasso Sea to European waters. You can also see migrations of the second-largest shark in the world right here in the UK.

The pelagic can support an abundance of life as its conditions change dramatically throughout the water column depending on depth, pressure, temperature, light intensity, salinity and oxygen concentrations. Interactions between these chemical and physical forces alter biological conditions too. The deeper you go, the harder it is to survive.

BLUE SHARK
Prionace glauca

Blue sharks migrate into our waters every summer, and although usually seen offshore, they occasionally come inshore for a closer look. Their top side is adorned with a beautiful iridescent blue colouration that shimmers in the sunlight as their sleek, torpedo-shaped bodies move through the ocean. It's unclear why blue sharks return to the UK year on year. Marine biologists believe they follow the Gulf Stream here from the Caribbean in search of food, and potentially a mate, before returning following the Atlantic North Equatorial Current. Blue sharks are sadly one of the most heavily commercially fished shark species on the planet, and their populations have experienced dramatic declines in recent decades, and they are now classed

as Near Threatened on the IUCN Red List of Endangered Species. They occur offshore from south-west England, alongside Wales and Ireland in the Celtic Deep, but you usually need to take a trip out with a responsible wildlife operator to get a glimpse of these magnificent animals.

THRESHER SHARK
Alopias vulpinus

With their whip-like tails, thresher sharks are hard to mistake and are often associated with the warm coasts of the Philippines rather than the south coast of the UK. Yet every summer, thresher sharks migrate to feed in UK waters. As with many species in the ocean, their distributions are undergoing changes due to environmental conditions and human pressures, so it is difficult to pinpoint their range, but at time of writing they are most commonly observed from the coasts of south and south-west England, as well as in the Celtic Deep. Occasionally they have been spotted making tremendous leaps and bounds into the air. Thresher sharks belong to a group of sharks that have developed endothermic abilities to

warm areas of their muscles, which helps them to hunt in colder waters. Using their elongated tail fin, they herd small fish into tight shoals where they stun them with a whipping motion, making the fish easier to catch.

BASKING SHARK
Cetorhinus maximus

Trying to witness these gentle giants first-hand should be on everyone's wildlife bucket list. Reaching up to 11m in length, the basking shark is the second-largest shark globally, and you can encounter it right here in the UK. There is still a lot we don't know about these elusive animals. Science is uncovering more and more about them each year, with potential key breeding

sites being identified, such as the Claire Coast in Ireland where hundreds have been spotted in an aggregation. These enormous sharks are filter-feeders, feasting on zooplankton which they sieve out of the water using their gigantic mouths. Basking sharks migrate huge distances each year, and satellite tracking data has shown them to go as far from the UK as Newfoundland in Canada. But in the summer months, they migrate to our shores, and your best chance of seeing them is to visit Cornwall or the Isle of Man in England and the Inner Hebrides in Scotland. You may be lucky enough to spot one of these magnificent sharks from cliffs elsewhere in the UK, particularly around Ireland. To get closer views, you can take a trip with a reputable wildlife company. Basking sharks have been documented breaching in a similar fashion to their great white shark cousins, leaping high out of the water. This spectacular sight may be to remove parasites or to attract a mate.

MINKE WHALE
Balaenoptera acutorostrata

Although it is the UK's smallest 'great whale', the minke whale is nevertheless a sight to behold. If you're lucky, you may even witness it breaching clear of the water or lunge feeding near the surface. In all likelihood you will smell a minke whale before you see it, so if you notice a fishy smell in the air, keep a look out. These remarkable whales have huge voices too and can reach volumes of 150 decibels to communicate with other individuals over long distances. Found throughout the northern hemisphere, what we call the minke whale is technically the northern minke whale and is a separate population from its southern cousins. You will typically spot this species on its own, but occasionally, you may be lucky to see it in a small group 'gulp feeding' on schools of fish or krill. Gulp feeding involves the whales taking a massive gulp of fish and filtering

them from the seawater using the specially designed baleen plates in their mouths that are lined with bristle-like structures. You can spot them year-round from the UK, particularly in Scottish waters, although sightings are rare in the Southern North Sea and the English Channel.

HARBOUR PORPOISE
Phocoena phocoena

Harbour porpoises can be seen inshore in shallow waters and are easily recognisable with their small, triangular dorsal fin as it pierces the water's surface. If you're close enough, you may hear them coming up for air as their blowhole opens up to take a breath. Harbour porpoises are much smaller than other cetaceans (the collective name for whales, dolphins and porpoises) and have a stocky appearance with a rounded face and no beak. They must constantly feast on fish to generate enough energy to keep them warm in our chilly seas. Compared to other toothed cetaceans, harbour porpoises live fast and furious lifestyles. They are sexually mature much earlier and reproduce more frequently than other species due to their relatively short lifespans.

Harbour porpoises are regularly spotted within 10km of land as they visit shallow bays, estuaries and tidal channels of less than 200m depth so you have a good chance of observing them from our coastline.

ORCA
Orcinus orca

You may know them as 'killer whales' instead of orcas, but they are not taxonomically considered to be whales and are instead the largest species of dolphin in the world. They are also sometimes affectionately referred to as 'sea pandas' due to their colouration, which resembles the bamboo-eating bear. Their 'killer whale' name derives from orcas' tendency to target whales much larger than they are as prey, and their varied, opportunistic diet. They are incredibly intelligent animals with refined hunting strategies, and each family group uses a unique language to communicate. Orcas are rare to witness in the UK, although a small pod (group) lives in the Scottish Hebrides. The UK's only resident orca family comprises only eight individuals known as the West Coast Community. This pod is increasingly under threat, and with no calf being born within this group in more than 25 years, their future survival in Scottish seas is in jeopardy. You can learn more about this on page 75.

MOON JELLYFISH

Aurelia aurita

Moon jellyfish are present throughout the world's oceans and are the most common jellyfish in our seas. The moon jellyfish is around the size of a dinner plate and is recognisable by the four purplish circles visible through its translucent white bell, which are its reproductive organs. Amazingly, these animals are 95 percent water, possess no brain, blood or heart, and are entirely dependent on the ocean currents for their movements. They have short tentacles that drift below them in the water, which they use to entangle prey. Moon jellyfish are often spotted washed up on beaches, so you will likely encounter them during a trip to the seaside. Scientists have observed especially large abundances of moon jellyfish in areas where human activity like overfishing and pollution are prevalent. Perhaps our influence on the ocean is causing their populations to increase.

PORTUGUESE MAN O'WAR

Physalia physalis

It is a common misconception that these beguiling creatures are jellyfish. In fact, they're siphonophores – colonial hydrozoans (a class of

water-dwelling animal) made up of small animals called zooids, each with a specific function, such as feeding or breeding. Portuguese man o'wars reside on the open ocean's surface, mostly in tropical and subtropical seas, and are held afloat by gas-filled bladders. They are fearsome predators, catching small fish and crustaceans with their long tentacles, extending by as much as 30m. Their tentacles are filled with stinging cells known as nematocysts, which they use to deliver venom to kill their prey. They can wash up on our shores, especially after large storm events, as they have a crest-like structure on top that acts as a sail, and because they can't swim, they're completely under the mercy of the weather. If you encounter these bizarre creatures along our coastline, it's imperative that you do not touch them, as they can still deliver their painful venomous sting even after death.

ATLANTIC MACKEREL

Scomber scombrus

Atlantic mackerel are like streamlined silvery bullets, speeding through the water in unison. They must be in constant motion to absorb enough oxygen from the seawater to survive. Mackerel have beautiful tiger-like markings on their backs – similar to those seen on tiger sharks (which do not inhabit British waters) – and they glisten in the sunlight. These fish may live for up to 20 years, with females producing between 285,000 and 2 million eggs each spawning season, from roughly 2 years old. This large volume of eggs mean they all survive, as fish eggs are eaten by many other species in the sea, which is why they must produce so many to increase the odds that enough will survive. Mackerel turn up inshore as summer arrives, following the zooplankton and smaller fish, like sand eels, which are some of their favourite prey. They are commonly spotted around southern England in areas like Chesil Beach in Dorset. Handline-caught mackerel are a sustainable food choice for humankind, and they are also an important food source for many marine predators in our waters, such as whales, dolphins, seals and sharks.

The Infinite Blue

It would be impossible to detail the enormous breadth of marine diversity inhabiting our seas in one volume, especially as the scientific community is continually discovering new species. There are enough adventures to be had around the UK coastline to last a lifetime, and each time you venture to the sea, you may encounter a new species to add to your checklist. Whether you want to pull on a snorkel and jump into the cool waters to explore a kelp forest or use a pair of binoculars to watch seabirds soaring above the clifftops, trips to the coasts around our archipelago offer something to excite and fascinate everyone, whatever your interests.

But our seas have been put under pressure by increasingly intensified human activities, even though we rely on them for many things. Given our dependency on the ocean, it seems counterintuitive that humans have exploited it almost to the point of no return so quickly. For humanity and our ocean to thrive together, we must learn to coexist peacefully and extract only what we need from it, sustainably. Before jumping into how we got our seas into this mess, let's contextualise our intimate reliance on the big blue.

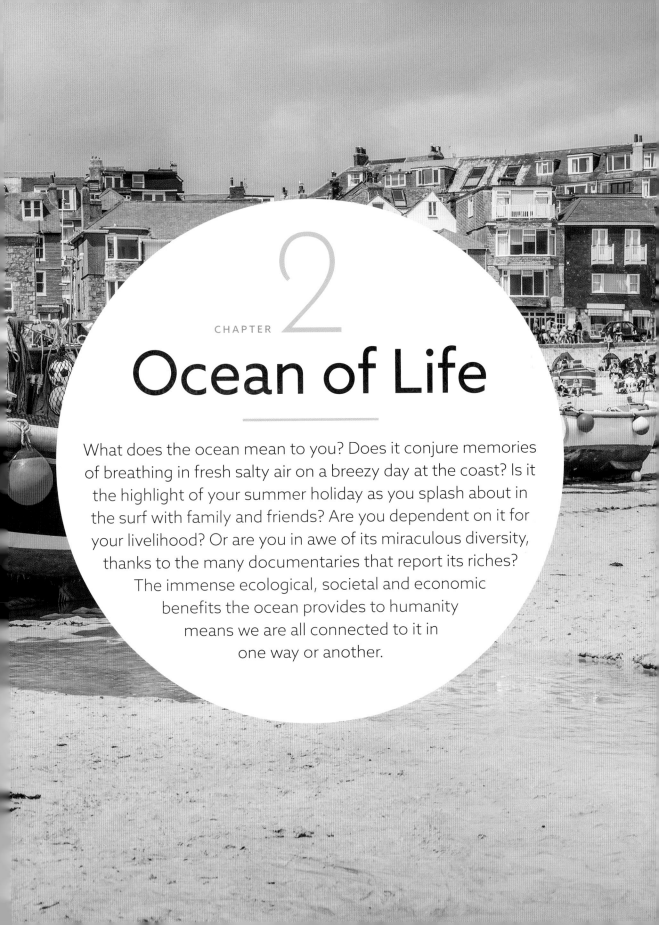

CHAPTER 2

Ocean of Life

What does the ocean mean to you? Does it conjure memories of breathing in fresh salty air on a breezy day at the coast? Is it the highlight of your summer holiday as you splash about in the surf with family and friends? Are you dependent on it for your livelihood? Or are you in awe of its miraculous diversity, thanks to the many documentaries that report its riches? The immense ecological, societal and economic benefits the ocean provides to humanity means we are all connected to it in one way or another.

Without our ocean, life as we know it would not exist. The term used by scientists to describe the life-giving goods and services our seas provide is 'ecosystem services'. To make it easier for scientists, economists and decision-makers (among others) to quantify their value to society, ecosystem services are categorised into four distinct groups: provisioning, regulating, supporting and cultural. A recent estimate suggested that UK marine biodiversity could be worth up to a total of £2,670 billion to the UK economy. In the context of ecosystem services, products obtained from the marine environment are classified as 'goods'; they include, for example, seafood and building materials such as sand and silt. On the other hand, 'services' are processes like climate regulation, coastal protection and carbon sequestration, which are vital for the functioning of the planet.

It might seem strange, cold or indifferent to try to classify every way that humans benefit from our seas in terms of goods and services, but in a capitalist economy, humans aim to ascribe value to our natural resources if they are to be deemed worthy of protection. And by doing this, conservationists can better demonstrate to decision-makers, economists and politicians, and indeed to all of us, the importance to society of safeguarding and restoring our marine environments.

Perhaps the most incredible thing about our ocean is how it unites us. The five oceans that dominate our planet's surface – the Arctic Ocean, Southern Ocean, Indian Ocean, Atlantic Ocean and Pacific Ocean – are all connected to make one enormous expanse of water, known as the global ocean. Even if you live hundreds of miles away from it, in a landlocked county, you are still connected to its life-giving

abilities. And yet it's often said that we know more about the surface of the moon than our ocean. Indeed, it is significantly easier to explore the dry surface of the moon than it is to navigate the Earth's vast, deep and wet oceans.

Providing for Society

We shamelessly exploit our planet's resources in our drive for ever more stuff and a perpetual pursuit for economic growth, and our oceans are not exempt from this exploitation. As we expand our horizons and develop technologies that allow us to utilise our seas sustainably, the concept of a 'blue economy' has emerged. The blue economy model improves human well-being and social equity through various ecosystem services while simultaneously reducing environmental risks and ecological scarcities. It prioritises the sustainable use of ocean resources for economic growth, supporting livelihoods and jobs, whilst improving ocean ecosystem health for all communities worldwide. Of course, any economic model requires a supply of goods and services, so let's learn about provisioning services.

Genetic Materials

Whether it's enzymes from sponges or compounds from algae to develop medicines and cosmetics, we describe the genetic information we can extract from the marine environment as 'marine genetic resources'. Marine genetic resources have already been used to develop treatments for cancer, microbial infections, and inflammation, and were even used to test for viruses, including coronaviruses. The deep sea is the final frontier on planet Earth, with many discoveries yet to be made. The marine genetic potential in

WHAT IS NATURAL CAPITAL?

Simply put, natural capital is all the natural resources we derive from our environment. This capital could be renewable resources, like energy and plants, or non-renewable resources, like minerals. Yet the natural capital that allowed the advancement of human society during the Anthropocene – the current period in our planet's history when the results of human activity began to influence the globe's biosphere and climate system seriously – is now experiencing catastrophic declines because of overexploitation. And increasingly, governments worldwide recognise the importance of understanding, conserving and replenishing natural capital when making political decisions.

TYPES OF ECOSYSTEM SERVICES

▶ **Provisioning services:** any tangible benefit that can be extracted from the natural environment. Examples include food, drinking water, algae, natural gas and timber.

▶ **Regulating services:** typically processes that moderate natural phenomena, such as pollination, climate regulation, water purification, carbon storage and decomposition.

▶ **Supporting services:** these are services necessary for all ecosystem services to function. Examples include living organisms, oxygen production and water cycling.

▶ **Cultural services:** non-material benefits that humans derive from ecosystems such as spiritual enrichment, cognitive development, reflection, recreation and aesthetic experience.

this part of our planet is enormous. Yet, as discussed in chapter 3, deep-sea mining threatens to destroy this precious potential before science even fully discovers it.

Renewable Energy

Renewable energy will be the key to fighting the climate crisis. The risks associated with renewables – particularly those offshore – are far outweighed by the dangers of fossil fuels. Wind turbines may be an eyesore, but is there any worse eyesore than the sight of the ocean boiling alive due to a fractured oil pipeline? The oil spill in the Gulf of Mexico in 2010 was akin to a scene from a science-fiction movie; visceral, visual confirmation of the need to move away from fossil fuels. As the growing climate crisis becomes more evident, with the increase of severe weather patterns worldwide, the argument for moving to clean energy is strengthening. We must reduce our reliance on fossil fuels and embrace inexhaustible energy sources instead.

Harnessing the natural power of the planet seems at face value to be a no-brainer. At any one time, the Earth is generating enormous wave, wind and geothermal power – and the best part is that they're infinite resources. The waves will crash, the wind will blow, and the Earth's crust will boil. On the flip side, fossil fuels are a finite resource. They are also hurtling us toward the single biggest ecological crisis to face our global community, causing environmental havoc along the way. Vast oil spills suffocate marine life. Heavy machinery rips through the landscape in search of fuel deposits. And great plumes of emissions invade the air we all breathe, diminishing its quality. There has to be a better way, a greener way.

Harvesting renewable energy from the ocean is an emerging industry with enormous potential to mitigate climate change by supplying clean energy that reduces greenhouse gas emissions. It works by harnessing the energy from the movement of water in estuaries and large rivers, the movement of waves in the open ocean, and collecting the energy from temperature and salinity gradients in the ocean. Marine renewable energy also includes ocean-

based wind power. The UK Government project that offshore wind will produce more than enough electricity to power every UK home by 2030. And at the time of writing, the largest offshore wind capacity in the world is being built at Dogger Bank off the east coast of Yorkshire. As we strive to meet our global commitment to net-zero carbon emissions by 2050, renewable energy will be crucial for our green strategy. It will also provide thousands of jobs as much of this investment into renewable energies will be delivered by the UK Government and industry to communities in desperate need of a social and economic invigoration. There are some drawbacks associated with specific renewable energy sources, which I will investigate later.

Fisheries

The fishing industry touches many facets of our lives, from cuisine to architecture, cultural identities and even décor. We have a somewhat romanticised relationship with the fishing industry, perhaps because it has been part of the fabric of our society for so long. We depend on healthy fisheries for the food they provide, the livelihoods they support and the cultural identity they bestow, alongside a range of ecological benefits. Healthy fish stocks remain the basis of the many benefits we derive from the fishing sector. Sustainably used seas are paramount, not only environmentally but also for maintaining local economies and people's livelihoods. After our exit from the EU, the UK Government created new laws known as

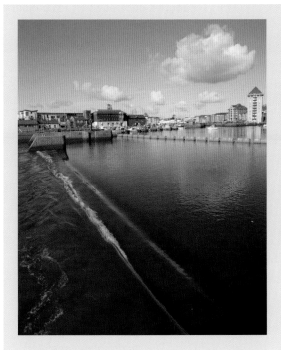

TIDAL POWER IN THE UK

Tidal barrages are located on powerful estuaries in the UK like Swansea Bay, the Mersey, the Severn. Tidal power in the UK is estimated to represent 50 percent of Europe's tidal energy capacity. By 2050 the tidal energy sector could create 23,500 jobs and represent £76 billion of the global tidal energy market, making a solid case for its inclusion within the UK's green energy strategy. Tidal energy is not without its risks, though . The turbines used by tidal energy plants may threaten marine life by sucking them into their enormous rotary blades, and the noise generated by the turbines may also disturb species like cetaceans. Scientists and engineers are working hard to reduce its environmental impacts as much as possible.

the Fisheries Act, which gives the UK complete control of its fishing waters and requires all UK fisheries to meet new ecological and sustainability objectives.

COMMERCIAL FISHING

Today's UK fishing industry is a shadow of what it once was. Due to overexploitation and habitat destruction, fewer fish in the sea provide smaller catches and support fewer livelihoods on land and at sea. Today, around 12,000 people – the same number that were provided work in the Scottish town of Wick's herring industry (right) at the turn of the twentieth century – work in commercial fishing across the UK. This figure declines every year. Recruitment within the industry is challenging, as the attraction of a dangerous life at sea dwindles. Yet the commercial fisheries sector employs more than just the fishers themselves. It also supports a host of jobs within fish processing, marketing and the seafood trade. Our exit from the EU has been a struggle for these tradespeople, as two-thirds of UK seafood is exported, predominantly to mainland Europe and Asia.

The commercial fishing industry undoubtedly plays an essential role in society,

HERRING GUTTERS, WICK

particularly in sea-fishing ports like Brixham, Whitby, Peterhead and Grimsby, the latter once the largest port in the world. But to keep reaping the benefits from the sector, through food security, job security or the heritage value we derive from fishing, we must learn to live alongside our seas and not exploit them beyond sustainable limits. Our coastal waters can provide seafood for our population and economy long into the future if we harvest them sustainably and with the least environmental impact. As we move forward, we have a unique opportunity to re-evaluate fisheries management and take the steps needed to rebuild fish stocks and secure the future of the UK fishing fleet. But are we willing to take the short-term squeeze to receive the long-term gain?

RECREATIONAL FISHING

Sea angling is a popular pastime in the UK, with more than 500,000 people taking part in sea angling every year. Catch-and-release angling is preferred by most anglers and conservationists but catching and keeping for the table is also a sustainable way to fish, as anglers generally only keep what they need and the unintended catching of other species, or 'bycatch', is reduced to almost zero. Sea angling can be a fantastic way of sparking intrigue in our seas. Still, anglers must adhere to the best possible handling and fish welfare practices to give fish the best chance of survival on release.

Marine recreational fishing is about more than just catching a few fish. Participating in sea angling is also beneficial for mental health, encouraging participants to reconnect with the sea. The NHS is trialling angling as a treatment for particular mental health conditions. Recreational sea angling also supports local businesses in coastal communities across our nation. People flock from all over the country to hotspots like Cornwall to line the harbour with crabbing lines or head out on charter boats. So entrenched is sea angling within our culture that certain iconic locations such as Admiralty Pier in Dover (below) have been hosting anglers since the late 1800s. Holding immense respect and knowledge of our seas, anglers are the eyes and ears we need to monitor our coasts.

Regulating and Supporting the World

Our oceans are integral to regulating the physical systems on our planet, stabilising its conditions and allowing biodiversity to thrive. These regulating and supporting services are finely balanced feedback loops (see diagram below for some of these), and even the smallest disturbance has the potential to knock them off-kilter. These crucial services are reason enough to motivate everyone to do their best for the oceanic world. Our existence depends on the health of these systems.

Climate Regulation

Perhaps one of the most important services the oceans provide us with is climate regulation. Our oceans form a key component of the world's climate system. All five oceans constantly and collectively exchange materials and physical properties, functioning as a global ocean.

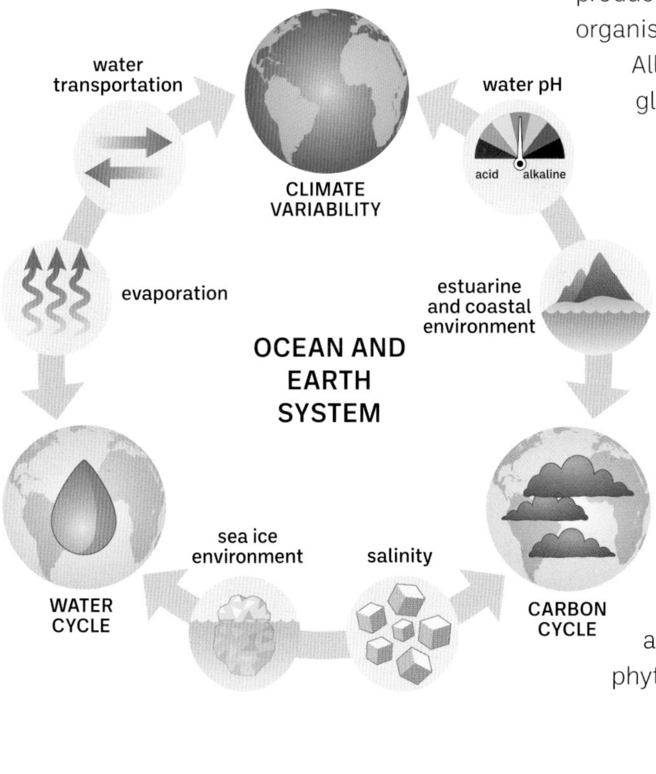

There is a significant latency period between atmospheric warming and ocean warming. The ocean has a large heat capacity, so it heats up and cools down very slowly. This means the full effects of the carbon we are pumping into our atmosphere today may not be apparent in the ocean for another 50 or 60 years. Remarkably, oceans store more heat in the top few metres of water than the entire atmosphere holds, including vast amounts of immense solar energy radiated by the sun. Experts predict that the global ocean can store up to a thousand times more heat than its atmospheric equivalent. This heat is gradually re-introduced back into the atmosphere over centuries.

A combination of physical factors feedback on one another, including surface winds, atmospheric and oceanic temperature and oceanic salinity. The interplay of these factors is an intricate dance that can easily be put off balance. Our oceans generate enormous upwellings, which occur when winds bring cool, deep, nutrient-rich water to the surface. This, in turn, promotes expansive biological productivity, creating an abundance of living organisms, all thanks to the nutrients.

All ocean currents are linked in a global conveyor belt of circulation that constantly works in tandem with the atmosphere, exchanging heat and redistributing it across the planet. Because everything on our planet is inextricably linked, it should come as no surprise that the ocean's living systems play an important role within global climate regulation. Its biological pump – the mechanism by which inorganic carbon is sequestered from the atmosphere and land runoff to living matter in the deep sea – can influence concentrations of atmospheric carbon dioxide. Minuscule phytoplankton and other photosynthetic

water transportation

water pH

acid — alkaline

CLIMATE VARIABILITY

evaporation

estuarine and coastal environment

OCEAN AND EARTH SYSTEM

WATER CYCLE

sea ice environment

salinity

CARBON CYCLE

organisms use carbon dioxide during photosynthesis, removing it from the water and allowing more to be absorbed from the atmosphere. More than half of the world's oxygen comes from such tiny photosynthetic organisms, which produce oxygen as a byproduct of converting carbon dioxide and water into glucose. Some of this carbon makes its way to the seafloor, sometimes thousands of kilometres down, where it is buried in the sediment, potentially for millions of years.

Carbon Sequestration

Our oceans are enormous stores of carbon. In the face of climate change, the ocean, as a store of 'blue carbon', provides a regulating service that is fundamental to shrinking the volume of carbon dioxide in our atmosphere. Worldwide, the marine ecosystems sequestering the most carbon are seagrasses, mangrove swamps, kelp forests and the pelagic (open ocean). These ecosystems have immense carbon-absorbing abilities: mangrove soils store 6.4 billion tonnes of carbon globally, and an average hectare of seagrass stores 7 metric tonnes of carbon. As dead marine life drifts to the seafloor and decomposes, ocean sediments also act as large stores of carbon, locking it away for thousands, if not millions, of years. However, as we continue to trawl and

OCEAN CIRCULATION

The ocean is constantly in motion. Currents like the Gulf Stream (indicated in the below diagram by the two red arrows to the immediate west of the British Isles), which gives such vigour to our coastline and is a contributing factor to our weather patterns, are shifting cool and warm water across the planet and bringing life with them. There are five major 'ocean gyres' that are comprised of the ocean's currents and formed by both global wind patterns and the Earth's rotational force.

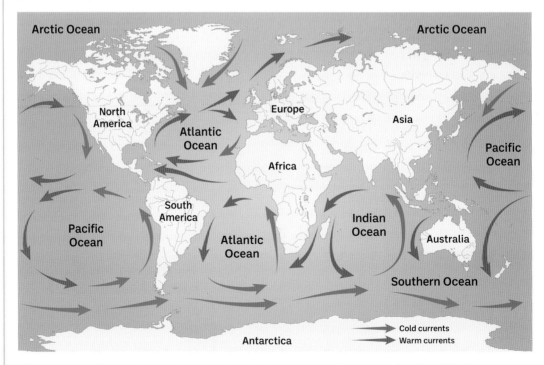

OXYGEN PRODUCTION

Scientists estimate that 50–80 percent of the Earth's oxygen comes from oceanic plankton – oxygen production is one of the vital supporting services the ocean provides

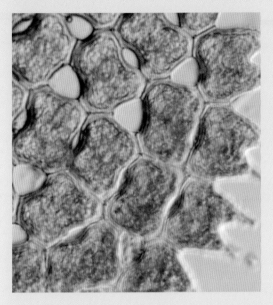

for all life on earth. Calculating the exact percentage is tricky because the amount of photosynthesising plankton within the ocean is constantly changing. Researchers use satellite imagery to aid their approximations, but this is unlikely to tell the whole story. The distribution of plankton within the global ocean also changes with the seasons and in response to environmental factors like the concentration of available nutrients and the temperature, so it is difficult to gauge the exact quantity of oxygen produced. Plankton are mostly invisible to the naked human eye, yet they represent more than 95 percent of total marine biodiversity. Staggeringly, the smallest photosynthetic organism on Earth – *Prochlorococcus* – produces up to 20 percent of the oxygen in our entire biosphere. That's more than the oxygen that all the tropical rainforests on land combined produce. Forests are often promoted as the lungs of our planet, and are a crucial component of the biosphere, but in reality, our lungs are blue, not green.

dredge the seabed, scientific research is identifying that we are releasing these precious carbon stores from the seabed, accelerating climate change. It may appear that offshore Marine Protected Areas are not protecting much, yet they also play an essential role in preventing carbon from being released into the atmosphere by heavy fishing gear.

Small yet mighty, coastal wetlands such as mangroves (right) are one of the most effective forms of carbon capture and storage on the planet. Covering less than 1 percent of coastal surface area, they store

WHAT IS BLUE CARBON?

Blue carbon ecosystems are another of our close allies in the fight against climate change. These ecosystems store carbon from the atmosphere for thousands of years in living and non-living material – such as calcium carbonate shells and ocean sediments – preventing it from entering the atmosphere. As organic material dies and new living material replaces it, dead material collects on the seafloor. There it begins to decompose. Over time, this material builds up and forms layers of sediment. If left undisturbed, it can store carbon for thousands, if not millions, of years.

more than 50 percent of the seabed's carbon reserves. While coastal wetlands are valuable stores of carbon in the UK, it is seagrass meadows, saltmarshes and kelp forests that are our primary holders of sequestered carbon. It is only recently that the actual value of these blue carbon ecosystems has begun to be understood. Astonishingly, scientists now recognise that coastal and marine ecosystems store up to six times more carbon than all types of terrestrial forest combined. In fact, researchers estimate that of the carbon that enters the ocean (around 80 percent of global carbon), around half is stored in marine blue-carbon ecosystems. As the central role these ecosystems play is further understood, it is becoming increasingly acknowledged that they could be a key ally in our fight against climate change. With this in mind, efforts to restore them must be properly funded and executed.

Water Cycle

Water: an essential substance for sustaining life. The global ocean covers about 70 percent of the planet's surface, making it by far the largest water reserve in the world. It plays a primary role in one of the most critical processes on Earth: the water cycle. This process, whereby water constantly circulates around the planet, has remained unchanged for billions of years. It is a regulating and provisioning service, and it is critical in maintaining the right conditions for life on Earth whilst also being the source of our drinking water.

As solar radiation from the sun warms the ocean's surface water, it has a fundamental role in the Earth's climate system. But it doesn't stop there. This process also contributes to the water cycle as the ocean's surface waters warm and evaporate. This water vapour is transported higher and higher into the atmosphere. The falling temperatures force it to condense into water droplets forming clouds. Once the atmospheric conditions

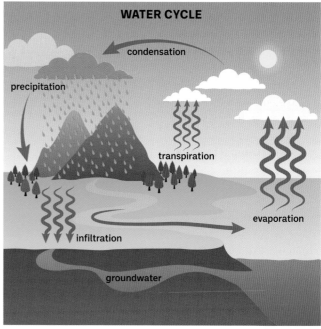

NUTRIENT CYCLING

Nutrients are the building blocks for growth, and lay the foundations for a healthy ecosystem to prosper. In marine environments, this is no exception. The ocean is a dominant player in the Earth's global carbon and nutrient cycles. These cycles are vital regulating and supporting services sustaining all life on Earth, and are significant to our planet's climate regulation. Everything is connected. Scientists refer to carbon and nutrient cycles as biogeochemical cycles – where chemical and other non-living (abiotic) elements are transferred between living (biotic) systems within the environment through processes like respiration and assimilation (the intake of nutrients as food). So, what is driving these crucial cycles? Marine microorganisms – especially zooplankton and phytoplankton – are the most valuable players. Exchanges between the Earth's spheres – the biosphere, atmosphere, cryosphere, hydrosphere and lithosphere – are continually swapping substances and elements between different systems within these cycles. For example, this could be atmospheric nitrogen being transferred to the soil by plants or organic carbon returning to the soil when an animal dies. It's important to remember that these natural forces can never create or destroy chemical substances, so they are continually being recycled or stored somewhere within the planet.

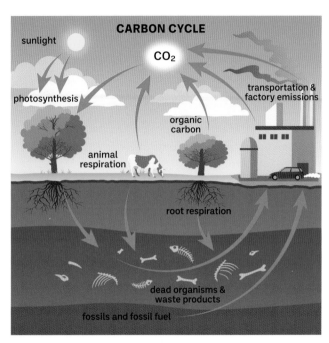

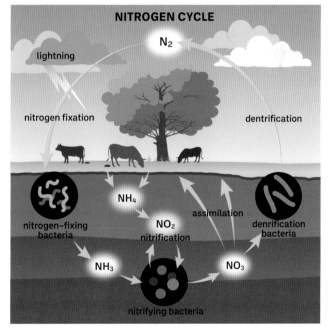

allow the cloud to reach saturation point, these droplets return to the Earth and seas as precipitation, like rain or snowfall.

As the ocean continues to warm, the evaporation rate accelerates, contributing to more frequent extreme weather events like cyclones and even droughts, when the distribution of water becomes more concentrated in some regions and less in others. There is a finite amount of water on the planet. It may take thousands of years, but every single droplet on Earth has been transported across the world by the global water cycle and ocean circulation.

Water Purification

Naturally improving water quality by filtering the nasty additions like pollutants, our biogenic reefs, as introduced in chapter 1, are water purification royalty. This essential supporting service enhances the quality of marine environments for all life to thrive. Blander in appearance than their coral counterparts, biogenic reefs are, in fact, vibrant living entities, and they perform an essential role in processing nutrients from the seawater into the benthic (seabed) environment below. Astoundingly, marine biologists estimate that an area of mussel bed (below) the same size

as a tennis court – the equivalent of around 400,000 mussels – can filter the equivalent of four Olympic-sized swimming pools of seawater per day.

Although we have lost vast swathes of the biogenic reefs along UK coastlines, there is fantastic work being done by university researchers, conservation organisations and grassroots projects to rewild our seas with vibrant oyster beds once again.

Seagrass and saltmarsh environments can also improve water quality, filtering water and reducing the influence of nasty eutrophication (nutrient concentration, which causes algal blooms such as the one pictured above, choking out fish and other species) within estuarine and coastal systems. They do this by acting as sinks for pollutants, sediments and other organic materials from the wastewater discharged into the sea, enhancing the value of coastal habitats.

Coastal Protection

As the oceans rise and the severity of weather patterns increases, natural coastal protection is one of our greatest allies in adapting to the impacts of climate change. Sadly, we increasingly witness and some of us experience the devastating impact of severe weather events with each passing year. The ocean is one of the most potent forces on the planet. As serene as it can be, it is also ruthlessly cruel.

With its boggy marshes and dynamic dunes, our magnificent coastline is a natural buffer against severe weather and rising sea levels. It stabilises sediment and protects coastal human populations and property. The vegetation found on saltmarshes and in seagrass meadows can dissipate wave action, reducing the impact oncoming tidal surges can have on property and lives. Rocky reefs also work in tandem with seagrass meadows to absorb wave action and diminish the impact of tidal surges.

At current rates of decline, scientists have estimated that saltmarshes and seagrass meadows worldwide have experienced a global 25–50 percent reduction in surface coverage since the 1980s. This reduction will expose coastal communities to flooding. It is in our interests to rewild these crucial ocean habitats for a range of reasons. For politicians, one of the most necessary is easing the economic and social costs that will result from severe tidal and weather events.

The need to protect our coasts should motivate us to work in harmony with our natural world rather than against it. For little investment, these unique habitats offer a nature-based solution to some of the world's most pressing problems. That's the best part: If we protect our coasts, they will protect us, and if we look after the ocean, it will look after us.

Breeding and Nursery Habitats

For fisheries to provide the socio-economic benefits upon which so much of our society depends, directly or indirectly, healthy fish stocks are vital. Ecologically speaking, breeding and nursery habitats are crucially important. But they are also critical in providing a foundation for a sustainable fishery. Without productive and sheltered habitats in which young fish can grow, there is a risk to future populations. These areas provide refuge and protection from predators and rough currents as marine life matures. For example, young plaice in their first year live mostly in very shallow water and can often be found in sandy tidal pools.

Breeding and nursery habitats are usually located within coastal habitats such as seagrass meadows (top of page 56) and kelp forests, but they also occupy estuaries.

SALTMARSH OR SEA WALLS?

As we continue to feel the effects of climate change, it's becoming more important than ever to have sufficient coastal defences in place to protect vulnerable coastal communities. But engineering solutions such as boulder barriers and concrete seawalls are expensive to install and maintain. What if there was a cheaper solution that required minimal effort to sustain? Nature-based solutions like saltmarshes may hold the answer. Scientists have identified that saltmarshes may reduce wave height by up to 80 percent and prevent soil erosion, providing stronger coastal resilience to severe flooding and reducing erosion caused by incoming wave action. Saltmarsh is also a valuable sink of blue carbon, so it could equally be an ally in reducing the effects of climate change by sequestering carbon from the atmosphere.

Juvenile sea bass, for example, depend on estuarine nursery grounds for the first six years of their lives. Without sufficient protection for these areas, the young fish are at risk of becoming bycatch within commercial fisheries. And while we have a good picture of where the most important breeding and feeding grounds are for some species, we don't have it for them all. We can always use more data to improve our current understanding. Data, such as the size, abundance and distribution of scallops (below), is crucial for fisheries managers and conservationists. In its absence, we encourage

use of the precautionary principle: protecting areas we think may be vital breeding and nursery grounds while we accrue the evidence we need to prove it, therefore ensuring the safety of future generations.

Culture Crafters

Are you calmer when you spend time at the seaside? Do you feel deeply connected to the coast? Perhaps you consider it a core part of your identity? Cultural services are all the elements that an ecosystem provides that are not material. Whether you enjoy them recreationally, appreciate them aesthetically, achieve physical or mental wellbeing from them, or perhaps feel a sense of spiritual significance at the coasts, these elements combine to foster a sense of place and a societal value we consider essential for human health and wellbeing. In our economically driven world, we often ascribe value to objects. Increasingly, however, social scientists offer evidence for the other types of value that our seas provide to society.

Health and Wellbeing

Do you feel happier around the water, less stressed and more connected to the world? The concept of a 'blue mind' within marine social science was first coined by American marine social scientist Wallace J. Nichols, who demonstrated that interacting with water makes humanity happier, more connected and better at what we do. A 2019 study by researchers at the University of Exeter also highlighted that people who live near the ocean are 22 percent less likely to develop depression and anxiety symptoms than people who stay inland. It seems more than a coincidence that many of us have a compelling urge to head to the seaside when the sun shines. The coast makes us happier. It relaxes us and makes us feel more grounded, more content with our lives and more at ease with our surroundings. Take a moment to close your eyes and imagine the warmth of the sun on your skin and the sound of waves peacefully lapping against the shore. You may unwittingly find yourself adding a soundtrack of a lone gull interrupting your attempts at mindfulness. Even so, I bet you feel better.

Scientists have proved that the sound of the ocean is so relaxing it alters our brain patterns. That's how powerful it is. People who use 'blue space' – areas along the coast or around lakes – are happier than those who do not spend time around water, and experience other psychological and social benefits. Scientific research indicates that spending time in blue spaces evokes more restorative feelings than spending the equivalent time in green spaces such as parks, forests or community gardens. And research has shown that the colour blue evokes feelings of peace, relieves stress and improves mental wellbeing.

Interacting with bodies of water is not only beneficial for our mental health but also our physical wellbeing. Research at the University of Exeter identified that people who live on or near the coast are typically more physically active, for example walking and swimming. Spending time close to the sea also promotes better sleep, increases levels of physical fitness and can even give you healthier skin. Inhaling salty sea air floods your brain with higher oxygen levels as the negative ions in sea air accelerate your body's ability to absorb oxygen and balance your serotonin levels, which can lead to a better night's sleep. As a result of splashing around in the waves, your skin is likely to improve. Seawater is a salty mixture rich in minerals, like magnesium, chloride, potassium, iodine and sulphur, which have all have anti-inflammatory effects.

Spending time in, on or by the ocean has so many benefits for our health. For ocean addicts

like me, the benefits I can gain from spending time at the coast are reason enough for me to want to protect our seas. Unfortunately, there are huge disparities between different communities and their access to blue space. Those from ethnic minorities and socio-economically deprived communities have unequal access to the many benefits the coast provides. With increasing scientific evidence to back the overwhelming mental and physical health benefits associated with spending time beside the sea, it's vital that we collectively improve access to blue spaces for all groups within society. Seeking to defend the ocean begins with establishing a connection with it. For us to succeed in ocean protection, we must ensure everybody can dive into its riches.

Tourism and Recreation

We all love to have fun in the sun, the sand and the sea. Whether you enjoy a trip to the coast for bird and whale watching, heading out to sea to catch a few fish or crawling around rockpools looking for underwater minibeasts, there is plenty of fun to be had beside the seaside. Simply acknowledging that there is a boundless expanse of water out there with infinite discoveries waiting to be made offers enough appeal for many. Spending time in the sea can

also allow us to learn a new skill such as scuba diving and develop personally by challenging ourselves to do this.

With more and more Marine Protected Areas (MPAs) popping up along our coastline, the opportunities for sustainable tourism also rise. MPAs alone are estimated to provide £3.9 billion in services to the UK economy and research suggests the presence of a Marine Protected Area can improve business three-fold. A 2019 report found that direct boating tourism adds more to the UK economy than the film, agriculture, forestry and fishing industries individually. The sector has created close to £6 billion in sales from boating-related tourism, a 65 percent growth since 2013, with 62,200 new jobs created in five years – and that's just the boating sector. In some coastal communities, particularly in Cornish locations like St. Ives and Newquay, over 50 percent of jobs are dependent on tourism.

Due to the global pandemic of 2020 we all spent more time on our home soil, and uncovered gems that have been on our doorstep the whole time. Many of us realised we don't need to fly halfway across the world to experience glorious sandy beaches and beautiful blue waters, which was fantastic for coastal communities that depend on tourism.

SHARK HUB UK: ANGLERS AND SCIENTISTS, TOGETHER AS EQUALS

Never has there been a more exciting time for UK shark science. We are observing a noticeable increase in shark encounters in our waters, providing us with an opportunity to understand these incredible animals better. Shark Hub UK is a collaborative partnership between the Angling Trust, the Shark Angling Club of Great Britain, the Sportfishing Club of the British Isles and scientific researchers at Bournemouth University, the University of York and Plymouth Marine Laboratory. Through its work, the coalition aims to support the recreational shark angling community with its development and to engage sea anglers in shark research. By working together, the team of anglers and scientists are paving the way for a sustainable future for UK sharks and deepening our understanding of these elusive predators.

Supportive Seas

We are all reliant on the big blue for one reason or another. It's therefore in all our interests to invest in its conservation – mainly for the oxygen we breathe! The blue economy is a growing sector, with experts suggesting that by 2030 it could outperform the growth of the global economy. In particular, an increase in marine energy, marine biotechnology, coastal tourism, transport and food production sectors could provide dramatic growth, offering many development and employment opportunities.

But marine ecosystems are some of the most heavily exploited worldwide. It makes little sense that the support system that gives life to us all is the same system that we are brutalising. A healthy, wildlife-rich marine environment should form the foundation of our economy, as society draws on many of its strengths and attributes. Maintaining the health of our seas and allowing damaged habitats and declining species populations to recover while ensuring the sustainable exploitation of our natural capital is the only way to ensure it can support future generations.

CHAPTER 3

The Threatened Blue

It is a surprise to many people that British seas are as fabulous as they are. As a result, our waters are often overlooked and undervalued. But, as we revealed in the previous chapters, our coastline is home to a wealth of diverse ecosystems. Our seas are also the lifeblood of coastal communities. Yet their exploitation can come at a high cost.

Across the world, our marine environment is experiencing unprecedented change. And in truth, it's terrifying. It can be challenging to comprehend the interconnectedness of our planet and the scale at which environmental change occurs. Take our global ocean, for example. Whilst the physical, chemical and biological forces powering it are mighty, so is our impact upon them. As the human population has dramatically increased, so has our appetite to consume, particularly within Western society. With more of us on the planet, humanity is encroaching on the natural world like never before to quench our thirst for resources and develop land for settlements, food production and other industries. In the process, we destroy more habitats, remove vast biodiversity and intensify climate change. We are experiencing the sixth mass extinction: a climate crisis and ecological breakdown.

Despite the beauty beneath the waves today, our seas are a shadow of what they once were. Isn't it incredible to think that no one alive on this planet today has seen the sea the way the sea should be? Life off our shores should be abundant. Through historical archives, such as photographs and maps, it's possible to see what once was thriving off our coast. In decades gone by we used to catch more fish, and bigger fish, than we do today and more seabirds were seen flying across our skyline. The primary driver behind this decline is no mystery. Since the Second World War our industrial fishing fleets have multiplied and we've become smarter and faster at catching fish. For every 10 large fish that should be swimming in our oceans, there's only 1 today. Scientists warn that if we continue to do this, over 90 percent of all fish stocks will be overfished by 2050.

Not too long ago it was believed that the ocean was

invulnerable to damage and was an infinite resource for us to exploit, yet the rate of degradation of the ocean in the last half a century alone has been alarming. Between 1970 and 2021, the World Wildlife Fund Marine Living Planet Index (LPI) identified a 49 percent decline in marine mammals, birds, reptiles and fish. In 2020 we also received heart-breaking statistics, including a 70 percent decrease in shark populations worldwide, with northern right whales being one of many species on the brink of extinction. In the UK, we have a terrible habit of contextualising the destruction of our natural world as a phenomenon that is only taking place abroad, stereotypically in the global south – a broad term that typically refers to Central and South America, Asia, Africa and Oceania denoting regions that are often, but not always, low-income and politically or culturally marginalised – despite most environmental change being fuelled by consumerism in Western society. Yet, to date, the UK has lost 95 percent of its oyster reefs, 90 percent of its seagrass and 85 percent of its saltmarsh – all of which are essential habitats for species diversity and carbon storage, vital in the fight against climate change. The North-east Atlantic waters – covering the Mid-Atlantic Ridge in the west to the North Sea in the east, and from the North Pole down to the Azores – around the UK have also been declared as a hotspot of threatened fish species, according to the European Red List of Marine Fishes published in 2015. Seabirds like kittiwakes and razorbills also face an uncertain future as storm surges and severe weather patterns intensify, their prey populations experience range shifts and sea temperatures rise. The demise of our ocean and its biodiversity is very much on our front doorstep.

In nature, it's rare for biodiversity to decline on its own. All species have evolved to thrive in a delicate balance with one another. So, these observed declines are undoubtedly caused by a single threat, or mixture of threats, driven by human activity. As the human population has exploded, we have replaced wild animals with domesticated ones, and the combination of humans and domesticated animals now accounts for 96 percent of all mammals and 70 percent of all birds on Earth. There's very little wild left.

In this chapter, I will introduce and explore these threats. Change is happening now. This is no longer a scientific prediction or a computer model; we are watching our planet fade with our own eyes in real time. We dredge the seabed, exploit its marine life and discard our waste into it at a rate that defies belief. Fish stocks are being depleted, wildlife is competing for space with human developments and pollution suffocates species as they fight to survive in an ever-changing world. Many factors are driving the loss of life in our global ocean, and it's important that we don't view them in isolation. The ocean is our lifeforce and yet we continually abuse it with very little regard for future generations that will depend on it.

A Changing Climate

When writing about the threats facing our ocean, it's impossible not to write about climate change. And yet for many of us it's not the first thing we think of when pondering the challenges facing our seas. We tend to focus on tangible issues like plastic first, rather than the looming risk of warming and acidifying waters. Just by its very nature, climate change is hard for us to grasp as a concept. It is gradual, with change taking place over decades, and many of us can't physically see its drivers – fossil fuels – or the process of greenhouse gases accumulating in the atmosphere. Other threats like plastic are palpable, and we can physically see ourselves reducing our use of single-use

plastics and subsequently there being less on our beaches. This gives us a dopamine hit – a feel-good hormone – that reinforces behavioural cycles and can be attributed to the success of the plastic-free movement. But societal shifts in the name of climate change are much harder to achieve. It's also worth noting that only approximately 100 companies are responsible for roughly 70 percent of the world's carbon emissions, so much of the change that is required to fight climate change is needed by international corporations rather than everyday individuals like you and me. However, as you will learn later, that does not mean that everyday people are powerless when it comes to doing something about the climate crisis.

Although climate action has not yet been as successful as plastic action, it is no secret that we're amid a climate emergency. Scientists at the UK Marine Climate Change Impacts Partnership (MCCIP) have compiled evidence that clearly demonstrates that warming seas, reduced oxygen concentrations, ocean acidification and sea-level rises are already impacting the UK coast. Over time, these changes in marine chemistry and physical properties increasingly affect oceanic food webs. Here in the UK, global warming is causing climatic zones to shift by up to 5km annually, according to a report by Rewilding Britain, triggering range shifts in important species at the base of the food web such as sand eels (left) and sprats. This ultimately has ramifications for other species higher up the food web, such as seabirds like the Puffin, which depend on these fish for survival.

Change is also happening too fast for wildlife to adapt to their ever-changing environment, leading to 'biotic homogenisation' where species that are more generalist survive over those that are specialists. Yet, whether they're a generalist or a specialist, if a species cannot adapt to warmer temperatures or shift to a more tolerable climatic range, they are at great risk of extinction. Given the pace of climate change versus that of adaptive evolution, we will likely lose many specialist species.

KEY CONCEPTS

Biotic homogenisation: a process by which two or more species or communities become increasingly similar over time. This change may be genetic, phenotypic (an observable change resulting from the interaction of genes with the environment) or functional, and it often reduces diversity. This process is a significant component of the biodiversity crisis.
Generalist: a species that can feed on various things and thrive in multiple environments.
Niche: a role adopted by a particular type of organism within its community.
Specialist: a species that eats a limited diet and occupies a much narrower niche.

FIVE SPECIES AFFECTED BY CLIMATE CHANGE

▶ **Atlantic Cod:** Along with the threat of overfishing, climate change is likely to contribute considerably to the demise of this deep-sea dweller. Rising ocean temperatures are contracting the range of Atlantic cod, but also causing them to move north in search of cooler waters, which may result in local extinctions.

▶ **Puffin:** These beloved birds migrate to our shores to breed over the summer months; however variable and violent weather patterns have led to numbers crashing as nests are damaged and birds are killed in storms. Their prey is also moving northward in response to climate change, leading to birds starving to death.

▶ **Atlantic Salmon:** Salmon have impressive life histories. They spend most of their time in the Atlantic Ocean before returning to the river system in which they were born. For those migrating to the fresh waters of Scotland, the projected temperature changes are likely to result in reduced reproductive success (warmer waters increase their metabolism, using up more energy, which contributes to a weaker reproductive success) and could be lethal for Atlantic Salmon.

▶ **White-beaked Dolphin:** With approximately 80 percent of the European population of white-beaked dolphins located in Scotland, these agile cetaceans need cold waters to survive. They risk becoming locally extinct as warming seas push them to the fringes of their normal range.

▶ **Guillemot:** Guillemots are another of the many UK seabird species that are experiencing a heightened risk of extinction due to climate change as rising sea temperatures impact the entire food chain.

Warming Seas

Since the industrial revolution, humanity has been pumping high levels of carbon dioxide and other greenhouse gases into the atmosphere, thanks to the increased consumption of fossil fuels and a rapidly growing population. From the food we eat, to how we heat our homes, to how we choose to travel, everything has a carbon footprint based upon the carbon emissions it produces that contribute to the warming climate. As greenhouse gases accumulate in the atmosphere, the impact of the greenhouse effect grows as more and more thermal energy from the Sun is trapped and absorbed by the atmosphere. Although invisible to the naked eye, this trapped energy heats our planet, much like a greenhouse warms under the hot summer sun. We all have a carbon footprint that varies in size as a result of the choices we make in our daily lives and the society in which we live.

But why does climate change impact our ocean? Isn't climate in the atmosphere? The ocean plays a key role in regulating the global climate system. By absorbing over 90 percent of the excess heat from greenhouse gas emissions since the 1970s, the ocean has shielded humans from even more rapid changes in climate. Although it may not sound like a lot, global sea surface temperatures have risen by 0.7°C on average since pre-industrial times. Marine ecosystems are extremely sensitive, and even the slightest of changes can have enormous consequences for marine life. Corals, for example, can bleach with just a 1 or 2°C fluctuation in water temperature, expelling the tiny symbiotic algae they depend on for food and consequently dying if the water temperature doesn't return to its normal range. Scientists currently predict under a number of different climate change scenarios that our global ocean will warm between 1.2–3.2°C, depending on how much we can curb our emissions, by the end of the century.

More evidence is emerging all the time of the effects of climate change being felt within our ocean already, and increasingly accurate computer models are predicting what is yet to come. Corals are bleaching, cold-water fish species are declining, and those currently at the equator are moving toward the poles as their native waters warm up. As a result, we will likely encounter different species along our shores over time. For example, scientists predict sand tooth tiger sharks and scalloped hammerhead sharks may one day be a common sight in UK waters. It's also theorised that the higher frequency of encounters with Atlantic bluefin tuna and other apex predators that we are currently experiencing is associated with a warming ocean.

Warming seas will also impact the humans that depend on our ocean. Many commercially valuable fish stocks are undergoing range shifts as they change their distribution in response to a warming sea, and this is having enormous consequences for the livelihoods of local fishers – especially those whose small vessels cannot venture further out to sea in search of fish. For example, since the 1990s scientists have monitored traditionally southern fish species moving into the cooler waters of the North Sea, providing new opportunities for fishers based in the North, but negatively impacting those in the South. While fisheries' productivity in particular is likely to be impacted, for reasons I will introduce later, we must view fisheries – and climate change – holistically, as there are many drivers of change, all feeding back on one another.

Rising Seas

A 2015 study predicted that if the entire Antarctic ice sheet melted, sea levels could rise by as much as 58m. At current rates of global warming this is certainly possible in the future.

That said, whilst the melting of ice caps in the polar regions is typically portrayed in the media as the leading driver of sea-level rise, it is not the only one. Thermal expansion also has a role to play. As the ocean absorbs more heat energy from the atmosphere, it warms, and with this higher temperature the water expands, making sea levels rise as a consequence. Think of it like a domino effect, with one event triggering a series of other, related events.

As a nation made up of islands, the UK stands to experience huge impacts from sea-level rise. Current scientific projections from the 2017 National Climate Assessment estimate that by 2100 sea levels could rise by as much as 2.4m. In the UK, low-lying coastal areas such as those surrounding the Thames Estuary and the Humber Estuary are predicted by oceanographers to be submerged by the end of the century. Climate change-induced sea-level rise will also increase erosion, flooding, weathering and decay at coastal heritage sites.

Oceanographers predict that here in the UK we will experience more severe weather patterns as the climate and ocean warm, and storm surges, violent winds, flooding and even tsunamis are likely to batter our coastlines. These ruthless weather events will destroy infrastructure and cost lives if coastal defences are not strong enough. A report for the Government's Committee on Climate Change (CCC) in 2020 found that nearly 530,000 properties are at risk from rising sea levels along the UK's coast. By the 2080s, the same report found that up to 1.5 million homes will be at risk of flooding, with more than 100,000 homes at risk from coastal erosion. Undeniably, this will have overwhelming impacts on life as we know it, with some areas of our coastline vanishing under the sea.

Sea-level rise is a considerable threat, not only to human civilisation but also to wildlife and marine ecosystems. Many ecosystems like kelp forests and seagrass meadows are

RELOCATION, RELOCATION, RELOCATION

By 2045, north Wales could witness the end of a village that has existed for more than a century. The residents of Fairbourne could be the first community in the UK to be decommissioned and relocated because of climate change and the subsequent threat of rising sea levels. Fairbourne is a low-lying coastal village, and the cost of installing coastal defence infrastructure is considered by the local government as too high. It is a tragedy to ask people to relocate from a village where many residents have lived their entire lives, but as our seas continue to rise it is likely that we are going to see this becoming a common theme in many coastal communities.

dependent on light penetrating through the water column to allow them to photosynthesise. As sea levels rise, less sunlight can penetrate the sea surface to a sufficient depth, and the organisms that depend on these ecosystems for survival perish. Ferocious weather patterns also threaten to damage fragile habitats such as coral reefs, and can disturb the seabed, smothering habitats like rocky reefs in suffocating sediment.

Acidifying Seas

Ocean acidification is a deadly and silent product of climate change – largely invisible until it's too late. Absorbing vast amounts of carbon dioxide lowers seawater's pH, increasing its acidity and threatening many biological processes within the ocean. Over the last 100 years, scientists have monitored a reduction in ocean pH by 0.1 units worldwide. Similar to temperature rise, it doesn't sound like much, but this reduction equates to a 26 percent increase in global ocean acidity. By 2100, under a moderate emissions scenario, scientists project that ocean pH will be reduced

by another 0.2 units, having catastrophic implications for life in our seas. It is estimated that ocean acidification is taking place at a faster rate in UK seas than in the wider North Atlantic.

Species such as oysters (below) that rely on a calcium carbonate skeleton or shell will have a particularly tough time under these circumstances. This is because ocean acidification reduces the concentration of carbonate in seawater. Carbonate is a key

building block within the marine environment. Organisms like corals and planktonic species depend on it to form their shells and skeletons. As the ocean acidifies, the existing shells and skeletons of these organisms may also begin to dissolve, and these species may struggle to form new ones. As a result, creatures such as mussels and lobsters may be threatened with extinction, both locally and more widely. Filter-feeding species like horse mussels and oysters have a crucial role within the UK's seabed ecosystems. Under current modelling projects, it is feared that they will disappear from UK seas by 2100 due to rising sea temperatures and acidifying seas. Other unique ecosystems like deep-sea cold-water corals are also in trouble, with the UK MCCIP predicting that roughly 85 percent of these ecosystems will be exposed to acidifying waters by 2060. Acidic seas could result in the proliferation of invasive species, as well as significantly altering UK marine ecosystems. In recent years Florida rock snail, Atlantic pearl oyster and Columbus crab have all hitched a ride to our shores on plastic. Our ocean is becoming a difficult place for marine life to survive.

Running Out of Oxygen

If warming temperatures, rising sea levels and an acidifying ocean didn't seem like bad-enough consequences of climate change, then there is also a fourth deadly outcome. Climate change is also responsible for reducing the concentration of oxygen in our ocean. Warming sea surface temperatures result in less oxygen being dissolved in sea water at the ocean-atmosphere interface, also known as the sea surface, due to its heightened heat capacity. Warmer seas are less able to dissolve oxygen. Hotter oceans also equate to increased ocean stratification – the separation of water into layers, typically due to water density – resulting in less mixing and ventilation of sea water, making it harder for oxygen to penetrate deeper waters. This is because warmer water holds fewer oxygen molecules than cooler water as the water molecules have more energy and are moving around more rapidly. As a result, oxygen molecules can escape more easily and the concentration of oxygen decreases.

Oxygen is a fundamental element for the survival of aerobic marine organisms – those that respire using oxygen. Research published in 2021 identified that the expansion of climate-driven deoxygenated zones could make pelagic sharks, like the blue shark (below), more vulnerable to fishing pressures as their available habitat is compressed toward the ocean's surface layers. 'Dead zones' are rapidly appearing across the ocean

as it loses oxygen at an unprecedented rate, due to climate change and pollution incidents. The addition of high concentrations of nutrients from sewage and agriculture leads to algal blooms – the rapid growth of microscopic algae that can smother an aquatic ecosystem. Harmful algal blooms occur when there are sufficient nutrients, sunlight, warm temperatures and low ecosystem disturbance, and leads to dense patches of algae on the surface. When the algae decompose, oxygen is sucked out of the water, creating a dead zone below the surface. These events are often referred to as a 'red tide' in the marine environment. So-called ocean dead zones – regions with no oxygen – have quadrupled around the world since 1950, with the number of areas of low oxygen, predominantly in coastal areas, having multiplied tenfold.

Oxygen depletion also has implications for habitat quality, degrading habitats and, in some cases, causing their total demise. Scientists at the UK MCCIP project that the oxygen concentration in UK seas is likely to decline by more than the global average, particularly in the North Sea. Scientists are also learning more each year about oxygen minimum zones, which are locations in the global ocean where oxygen saturation in the water column is at its lowest. They are usually found between 200m to 1,500 below the surface. As climate change advances worldwide, oxygen depletion will undoubtedly advance across the global ocean, contributing massively to species decline.

A Polluted Planet

Humanity does a very good job of polluting, and in the modern era, pollution is increasingly dominating our seascape. Pollution is defined as the introduction of materials or substances to the natural environment that have an adverse effect. It comes in many forms –

CLOSING THE HOLE IN THE OZONE

Can we, as a global community, really come together to bring about the collective change needed to halt the climate crisis? It seems like an overwhelming task in the face of such challenges as international governments who refuse to agree, fossil fuel companies focused on profit, and climate change deniers who bury their heads in the sand. But we have enacted change on this scale before.

Fourteen years after we discovered that ozone-depleting substances, such as chlorofluorocarbons (CFCs), were damaging the ozone layer, governments implemented a global ban on these chemicals. The Montreal Protocol on Substances that Deplete the Ozone Layer is a landmark multilateral environmental agreement signed in 1987 by 197 countries. Since its introduction, the ozone layer has already shown signs of recovery, and experts anticipate it could be fully restored by 2050. The Montreal Protocol demonstrates that change of this magnitude is possible and offers hope for a global agreement on climate.

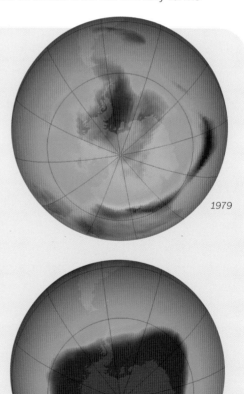

1979

2015

plastic pollution, sewage pollution, agricultural pollution, chemical pollution, noise pollution and light pollution – and is our unsavoury mark on the natural world.

Some types of pollution are harder to see than others. In recent years we have felt the effects of the *Blue Planet II* impact as more people have joined the plastic-free movement as a result of the natural history television phenomenon. Plastics are ingested by seabirds and entangle seals, ghost nets drift in the currents and ensnare migrating sharks, and animals from tiny plankton to gigantic blue whales take in microplastics. They appear to have infiltrated every aspect of our planet – both living and non-living. Plastics have a devastating impact on life in the global ocean, but they are by no means the only form of pollution wreaking havoc on our marine life.

Drowning in Plastic

Plastic is the buzzword on everyone's lips right now. It has overwhelmed our beaches (below) and suffocated our marine life. It is estimated that we dump 8 million tonnes of plastics into our ocean every single year – the equivalent of a lorry-load a second – although this figure is likely to be much higher. From macro-plastics like bottles and bags (top left) to microplastics like microbeads and microfibres, they permeate almost every aspect of our lives nowadays, from the food we eat to the air we breathe. Plastic has even invaded the furthest reaches of our planet – the deep sea. Scientists have concluded that there is probably no marine ecosystem left that has not been impacted by plastic pollution, after the discovery of microplastic ingestion by organisms in the Mariana Trench – more than 6,000m below the surface of the Pacific Ocean.

Where does all this plastic come from? One of the largest contributors to plastic pollution worldwide is plastic bottles, with an estimated 500 billion used every year. In fact, there are approximately 66 times more plastic bottles on the planet than people. Of course, it goes beyond plastic bottles and bags, although they are some of the major culprits. Surfers Against Sewage – a grassroots charity focussed on campaigning for healthier oceans and coasts

in the UK - conducted a 2021 study in the UK that confirmed up to two-thirds of all branded packaging pollution across the UK coastline could be traced back to only 12 companies, with Coca-Cola's bottles and cans leading the assault on our seas. Other common plastic offenders include fishing gear, like nets and lines, and bags, coffee cups, container lids, straws, food wrappers and foam fragments. In the UK, on average 5,000 plastic items are found per mile of beach. Worldwide, some areas of our ocean now contain six times more microplastics than plankton. Look around your immediate vicinity as you read this book: most likely you will be able to see several single-use plastic items.

Plastics are damaging materials, but by design they are also superb manmade materials that have enabled us to revolutionise medicine and technology. We have seen this in real time throughout the coronavirus pandemic as personal protective equipment (PPE) has been paramount in fighting infections and keeping people safe. Some plastics are necessary, but the vast majority, such as food

packaging (above), are primarily produced for our convenience rather than our health or safety. The very qualities that make plastics so useful, also make them a huge problem.

The dark consequences of our unhealthy addiction to this material occur during its disposal. The UK produces more plastic pollution per person than almost any other country, much of it single-use plastics like food packaging. Everywhere you go there are convenience food and drinks, single-use toiletries and quick cleaning products ready

HOW DOES PLASTIC BREAK DOWN?

Unlike biodegradable materials that decompose naturally, plastic does not break down this way and instead 'photodegrades'. Photodegradation is the process by which solar energy from the sun, in the form of sunlight, breaks down plastics into smaller and smaller pieces. As a result, they never leave the environment. Plastics can also be degraded by various other physical, chemical and biological processes, and, depending on the plastic material and its size, they can take a few decades to around 500 years to break down into microplastics or even smaller nanoplastics.

all marine debris found from surface waters to deep-sea sediments. There is now so much plastic in our global ocean that scientists have coined the term 'plastisphere' to refer to the plasticised marine environment and the biome it has produced. First described in 2013, scientists use this term to refer to organisms such as bacteria and fungi that colonise sea-drifting plastic, as well as the larger organisms like crabs and small fish, which may use plastic items as a raft to travel across the ocean (left). The most well-known concentration of plastic waste in our global ocean is the Great Pacific Garbage Patch, a plastic stew that equates to an area roughly twice the size of France.

for our one-time use and disposal. Where does all the plastic go when you or I have finished with it? Much of the UK's plastic waste is disposed of by shipping it overseas. Many of the countries that receive plastic waste, such as Malaysia, Turkey and Poland, are not equipped to handle its processing properly and therefore it is usually either burnt or sent to landfill, where it causes enormous problems environmentally and has consequences for human health. But the waste that isn't loaded off onto container ships continues its life in our plastic-soup seas.

For decades humanity has been mindlessly dumping our plastic waste into the ocean with no real thought for the consequences. Experts estimate that plastic makes up 80 percent of

Ingestion, entanglement and absorption are the main ways plastic impacts our wildlife, from soaring seabirds to schooling salmon. It's estimated that 100 million marine animals die from plastic pollution annually. In 2019 a dissection took place by the UK Cetacean Strandings Investigation Programme (CSIP) of a dead whale that had washed up on a Scottish beach. During this dissection scientists discovered approximately 100kg of plastic within the whale's stomach, including fishing nets and rope, packing straps, carrier bags and plastic cups. We will never know for sure, but ingesting high volumes of plastic pollution likely led to the whale's death.

Plastic is also a carrier of marine life, and can transport invasive species from one area of the ocean to another, causing potentially

GHOST FISHING

When fishing nets are lost at sea after a raging storm or stuck on the seabed, their fishing life doesn't end there. These nets continue fishing but in a new way: ghost fishing. This lost or abandoned fishing gear will continue to entangle marine life as it drifts with the currents. The commercial fishing industry uses various techniques to target different fish species so there are many kinds of ghost gear – from longlines of 100km or more to colossal nets that can engulf the seafloor. Fishing gear is predominantly made of plastic to ensure it is robust enough to endure harsh oceanic conditions. Although this is favourable for fishers, when their plastic fishing gear is lost, like other forms of plastic,

it will never fully degrade. Abandoned fishing gear is one of the leading causes of marine pollution today. The World Wildlife Fund estimate that at least 10 percent of plastic in the ocean originates from ghost fishing gear.

catastrophic damage to marine ecosystems. It has also entered the food chain, impacting human as well as marine animal health. For example, in 2016, researchers found that microplastic particles in food can damage organs and leach dangerous hormone-disrupting chemicals, known to affect immune systems, growth and reproduction. As apex predators of the food web, we are likely to be victims of our actions, polluting our bodies and the wider environment.

When looking at the statistics on plastic, it's easy to feel depressed. Less than a third of plastic here in the UK is recycled, and as our global population grows so will our demand for single-use plastic products – particularly in the wake of the global coronavirus pandemic. Even before the pandemic, plastic production was already forecast to grow 60% by 2030 and to treble by 2050 globally. This figure is now likely to be much higher. It's clear that society is heavily dependent on this seemingly indestructible material, yet through environmental awareness campaigns we also

know we need to do something about our reliance on it. A 2019 survey on UK plastic pollution measures revealed that 76 percent of respondents did not believe enough is being done to tackle the plastic pollution crisis. It is practically impossible to rid the world of plastic. Our attention must now divert to reducing our consumption of this manmade resource and valuing it more within society. Much of the change needed is required by governments and industry, but through using our purchasing power we can create consumer demand for eco-friendly alternatives. You can read more on solutions to the plastic crisis and practical steps you can take to reduce single-use plastic in your life in Chapter 5.

A Cocktail of Chemicals

Life in the ocean is subject to a toxic concoction of chemicals. These tend to be invisible killers that cannot be seen with the naked eye, but instead are looming in the water as a dangerous accumulating chemical cocktail. An estimated 80 percent of these chemical pollutants found in the seas originate from the land and make their way to the ocean by flooding into the sea after heavy storms. Toxic metals like arsenic, mercury and lead can be introduced in this way. But these chemicals do not solely originate from industry; they're everywhere. Household items like cleaning products contain PFAS (polyfluoroalkyl substances), plastic water bottles contain BPA (Bisphenol A) and even the pharmaceuticals we ingest make their way to the sea via our water system. Boats and ships also leak chemicals like engine fuel and anti-foulant paint that alter the ocean's chemistry. Fossil fuel extraction plants like offshore oil platforms can leak oil, and in the worst cases explode,

leading to catastrophic oil spills. The higher up the food chain you go, the more concentrated these pollutants become – this is termed 'bioaccumulation' – accumulating in the tissues of marine life, and us.

In many cases these chemicals have been banned for a number of years, yet they still circulate throughout the world and in some cases continue to be illegally produced or used until supplies run out. Endocrine-disrupting chemicals (EDCs) are one of the most common types of polluting chemical; they interrupt the hormonal system of organisms, which has ramifications for reproductive success. They have also been known to contribute to sex skews in certain fish species. An example of EDCs are polychlorinated biphenyls (PBCs). These industrial chemicals accumulate in the tissues of whales, dolphins and porpoises in UK and European waters in very high concentrations, despite being banned globally in 2004. While they are not fully understood, PBCs are likely to be highly toxic and yet another driver behind the population decline of these cetaceans. Another example of these endocrine-disrupting hormones is usually lurking in our beach bags. Oxybenzone and octinoxate are ingredients often found within sun creams as they are easily absorbed into the skin and don't leave a white residue behind. When we enter

WHAT IS BIOACCUMULATION?

Bioaccumulation is the process by which pollutants, like mercury, arsenic and other chemicals become more concentrated within an organism as they move up the food chain, which impacts all marine species. For example, the concentration of pollutants absorbed by plankton is relatively small; however, when a small fish like a smelt or a small crustacean like a prawn ingests ten plankton, the concentration of pollutants

multiplies tenfold. This cycle continues until it reaches the top of the food chain and species like sharks, whales and even humans, where the highest concentration of pollutants accumulates. It is unclear whether we can reverse the impact of chemical pollutants and subsequent bioaccumulation, although it appears unlikely. Our best bet is to stop dumping chemical pollution into our environment and cease producing chemicals as soon as we are aware of their potentially harmful impacts.

OUR CHEMICAL LEGACY

There is a pod of orca (or killer whales) living off the western coast of Scotland. They live in waters severely polluted by PBCs from industry – the chemical has been used extensively during the last century, for example in plastics and electrical equipment. As a result, the pod has been experiencing reproductive problems for 25 years. Over time, PBCs accumulate in whale tissue, and when researchers examined a female named Lulu from the pod that washed up on the coast, they confirmed it had PBC levels 100 times the threshold of toxicity. PBCs are also passed from mother to calf through their milk, so any calves this pod successfully

births die because the orca mothers are unwittingly poisoning their offspring. This pod's future is critically endangered, and researchers are concerned that the long-term toxic consequences of PBCs, which were banned globally in 2004, could decimate or wipe out as much as half the global orca population by the end of this century.

the water these chemicals leach into the water from our skin adversely affect the local ecosystem and its species' reproductive success. These are just two examples of the many hormone-disrupting chemicals disguised as everyday household objects.

Chemical fertilisers and pesticides we use across our farmlands (see page 74) to improve agricultural productivity are another harmful influence on our ocean. They often reach our waterways via surface runoff after heavy storms, but in other cases are actively discharged as waste products into our environment. Nutrient pollution within coastal waters upsets the delicate balance of nutrients within our seas. Scientists predict that by 2030 the global quantity of nitrogen in our global ocean due to chemical pollution will have increased by 14 percent since 1995. As discussed earlier, rapid increases in nutrients like this can lead to huge growths of algae,

SUPERCHARGING ANTIBACTERIAL RESISTANCE

Pharmaceuticals, including antibiotics, can also enter our waterways via sewage and agricultural runoff, and they are often hard to remove from water even when treated. Increased concentrations of these chemicals within our waters are a serious risk to humanity as they supercharge anti-microbial resistance (AMR), making infections harder to treat and leading to the creation of 'superbugs'. Worldwide, scientists have detected 113 pharmaceuticals in coastal waters. Prolonged exposure to these chemicals can cause bacteria to become resistant to them, and the impacts of this can be felt up the food chain, from tiny microorganisms like plankton to larger animals including humans.

resulting in algal blooms which deplete the ecosystem of oxygen. In turn, this causes hypoxia and death for aquatic life within these systems, not to mention the physiological impacts which may also take place as they accumulate within the tissue of organisms. Chemical pollution of any kind is all the more deadly for being an invisible killer within the ocean, with many of its impacts not being detected for decades.

Suffocating in Sewage

All rivers lead to the sea, and our rivers are in a dire state here in the UK. Data released from the Environment Agency in 2021 showed a 37 percent year-on-year increase in sewage discharges, with human waste flowing into our rivers for over 3.1 million hours and storm drains were released over 400,000 times in 2021, when they should only be discharged during severe weather such as flooding. This putrid pollution and human waste mixture suffocates our water-dwelling wildlife across our freshwater rivers and lakes, coastal estuaries and seas.

It's more than just human sewage that is the problem though. Within that waste are also microplastics from laundry water, chemicals found in plastics and cosmetics that can

SOUTHERN WATER SCANDAL

In 2021 Southern Water, a privately-owned water company in England, was fined a record £90 million for dumping untreated sewage into the sea. The Environment Agency discovered that Southern Water had been releasing sewage waste into some of the most protected marine environments in the country. The company released the equivalent of 371 Olympic-sized swimming pools full of untreated sewage into Southampton waters over a four-and-a-half-year period. This was a landmark investigation and prosecution within the water sector, and a defining moment after mounting public pressure.

disrupt hormone balances, and pharmaceutical residues from antibiotics we've ingested. It's a chemical catastrophe. Sewage pollution often includes chemicals from agricultural runoff like phosphorus that can lead to deadly algal blooms that kill huge numbers of fish and other wildlife by cutting off their oxygen supply. It is a deadly mixture that is disastrous for our environment.

As our population increases, we are producing more sewage waste and our archaic waste system is struggling to cope.

With climate change we will also experience an increase in the number of storms and their intensity, leading to more flooding events and more sewage entering our waterways. Enormous 'fatbergs' composed of fats and oils that we flush down the drain accumulate non-biodegradable products, like wet wipes. As they grow, 'fatbergs' block sewers, adding further pressure on our environment.

Blinding Lights and Deafening Sounds

Often overlooked, noise and light pollution are frequently forgotten when first thinking of pollution. The word 'pollution' evokes images of human waste, stinking rubbish piling up and infecting our environment, but it is more than that. Pollution effectively means something that is not meant to be where it is, and excessive noise and light within delicate ecosystems can be problematic for many species. It's estimated that 54 percent of Europe's coastline is affected by artificial light pollution, which is already having huge impacts on marine species by altering their behaviour. Here in the UK, rapid coastal development is taking place as people seek to relocate from urban areas to coastal towns, and coastal property becomes more expensive. As a coastal area becomes more populated it also increases its output of light pollution, which may have implications for coastal species. This is particularly an issue at night for animals or birds that rely on the cover of darkness to hunt or evade predators, and other species' habitats may be disrupted, such as resting seals and nesting seabirds.

The ocean is also naturally a noisy place.

OCEAN SUPERHIGHWAY

Shipping is integral to the day-to-day running of our maritime nation. Our 51 major ports import and export 95 percent of our goods, including almost 50 percent of our food supplies. As our population swells and our demand for resources grows, shipping traffic will need to expand. With this comes an increased risk of oil spills, heightened pollution and the chance of lethal collisions with marine megafauna like whales. The global ocean today is like a busy motorway that these gentle giants must traverse whilst attempting to avoid horrendous, life-threatening injuries that often lead to agonisingly slow deaths.

There is a symphony of sound taking place that marine creatures depend on for their survival, and to identify a mate, find food and navigate. It's getting noisier thanks to us, so much so that noise pollution from humans is now recognised as a leading threat to marine life. Sound is critical to marine life, as light penetrates only a few hundred metres underwater. Cetaceans rely on echolocation to detect their prey and for navigation, and many use clicks and songs to communicate with one another. Introducing manmade noise to the marine environment can drown out these natural sounds and disorientate these species. Scientists have estimated that increased artificial noise within the marine environment reduces the ability of cetaceans to communicate by approximately 60 percent. Seismic and military testing can also cause internal damage to whales and dolphins, and

POWERING OUR PLANET

The global ocean is an enormous powerhouse of natural, renewable energy. If humanity could harness the power of the ocean with its intense waves, powerful winds and ever-changing conditions, it would unlock an infinite source of renewable energy. Unfortunately, accessing this renewable energy resource is not without its risks, and engineers are increasingly discovering the impacts renewable energy technologies have on marine species and their habitats. Offshore wind farms, wave energy farms and tidal power plants are all forms of marine renewable energy that rely on turning rotary blades to harvest ocean energy via kinetic energy, which we use to generate electricity. Collisions with these blades can be deadly to marine life, such as seals, whales and seabirds. Scientists and engineers are currently experimenting with ways to produce noise to reduce the threat of collisions by warning wildlife of their presence.

Underwater noise from renewable energy structures may also drone out communications between animals, particularly between cetaceans, and may interfere with their echolocation, altering their natural behaviours. It can also cause life-ending injuries such as internal damage or permanent deafness if not adequately mitigated against. Introducing of these new structures in marine environments can also lead to sedimentation, interference with magnetic fields, and light pollution. Even the currents and wave patterns may also experience changes due to renewable energy structures interrupting the flow of water.

Wind farms are vital to our carbon-neutral future, but they must be designed with climate and nature in mind to reduce pressures on marine wildlife and our seas.

has been linked with mass stranding events. Oil and gas exploration operations often use air guns that could have an impact zone as large as 4,000km from the initial source point. The naval use of sonar has also been associated with a large number of whale strandings around the world, since a mass stranding event in Tenerife, the Canary Islands, in 2002. Whilst noise and light pollution are short-lived compared to other pollutants like plastics and chemicals, they are by no means less deadly.

Deep-sea Mining

Deep-sea mining is the process of extracting precious metals from the seafloor and could be worth £40 billion to the UK economy over the next 30 years. Although there is potential for these resources to be found within our waters, from a UK perspective most deep-sea mining is likely to take place within the UK overseas territories. The Ascension Islands on the Mid-Atlantic Ridge is one such identified hotspot. Technological advances, increased mapping of the seafloor and growing demand for precious metals are fuelling the desire to exploit the darkest depths of our seas. These metal deposits have the potential to fuel green energy such as batteries in hybrid cars. However, deep-sea mining can also be a deeply destructive activity – exactly the opposite of what we should be doing to our seas.

This is a new world so to speak, and so we have no idea of the true consequences for the deep sea. The deep sea itself is a relatively new frontier to science, with many questions remaining to be answered on its biology and ecology – scientists are discovering new species almost every time they venture down there! The pace of life in these dark depths of our planet is also infinitely slower, and so recovery from disturbance and damage is likely to take more time. We increasingly understand the role the deep sea and the seabed have in carbon capture and storage too, with disruption leading to the release of this carbon and accelerating climate change. Deep-sea ecosystems may also hold the secret to some of the world's most complex problems, perhaps holding cures for the deadliest of diseases like cancer. At this stage, it would be irresponsible for us to seek to destroy a fragile environment like the deep sea before we have a chance to fully understand it – have we learned nothing?

Disturbing the Flow

Around the British Isles, we are losing our marine and coastal habitats at an alarming rate. As our population grows and ages, more people may want to relocate to the coast. Meanwhile, as the wealth divide grows, more people from wealthy urban areas are seeking to buy a second home in our coastal regions, especially Cornwall. This increased

development and coastal squeeze, twinned with the impacts of climate change and heightened pace of coastal erosion, are accelerating the rate at which we are losing these delicate ecosystems. The UK National Ecosystem Assessment (UK NEA) indicates that UK coastal habitat has reduced by 16 percent since 1945, which may not sound like a lot but when you break it down into individual ecosystems like seagrasses and oyster beds, of which we have lost over 90 percent it shows what damage has been done. The same 2011 report predicts that by 2060 the UK will lose another 8 percent of coastal habitat, most of which will have been through coastal property development.

As more people descend upon the coastline, particularly in the summer months, human interactions can present challenges for marine wildlife. Disturbance is one of these challenges, and is a broad term scientists use that encapsulates a range of temporary changes in environmental conditions that can disrupt natural behaviours and processes. In this context, disturbance refers to human behaviour disturbing or harassing wildlife. Disturbance can cause a range of responses in the wildlife it affects, such as reduced feeding activity, reproductive difficulties, increased stress and diminished energy levels, all of which can be problematic for marine life in an ever-changing world.

Wildlife disturbance isn't just caused by the usual culprits like noise pollution, fishing gear or boat traffic. Tourists and recreational visitors to the seashore can also have huge impacts on

wildlife through harassment and disturbance, as seen in recent times with the massive amount of public attention received by 'Wally' the walrus, who occupied our shores for several months. Disturbance can be a particular problem when getting in the water with wildlife like basking sharks, or following dolphins and whales on a boat, and is one of the leading risks of ecotourism operations. Even coastal walkers can encroach upon seals resting on a beach, which causes them to become stressed and return to the sea without having sufficiently rested. In 2021 Cornwall Wildlife Trust reported that marine disturbances along Cornish coastal areas such as Newquay and Falmouth have more than tripled since records began.

Even though many of our UK species are protected from disturbance through legislation and policy that enables enforcement authorities to prosecute those found guilty of upsetting our wildlife, it's important to follow best practice when interacting with marine species to minimise disturbance. Where applicable these can be found on relevant environmental non-governmental organisations or responsible ecotourism operator websites. There is more information on this in Chapter 6.

Trading Marine Wildlife

Worldwide wildlife crime and trafficking are a substantial threat to biodiversity. Species like seahorses, sharks and eels are illegally caught and transported across the world

because of their high value in the traditional medicine market, in the tourist souvenir industry and for traditional delicacies like shark fin soup. It's easy to assume that wildlife crime is another issue that countries face on the other side of the world and not something we actively play a role in here in the UK. But sadly, there are many examples of marine and coastal species being trafficked from our shores as part of the global wildlife trade. Many of these species are protected by international legislation such as CITES – the Convention on International Trade of Endangered Species – and their trade on the black market is highly lucrative. While not a marine species, the European eel (above) spends part of its lifecycle in the Sargasso Sea before making its way back to UK rivers in an immense migration to spawn. Sadly these rivers are also the epicentre of wildlife crime in Europe. As the species has become critically endangered, illegal trafficking has increased, most notably to Asia as part of a multimillion-pound industry. The UK is not only a source for illegal wildlife trade and crime, but also more often than not a middleman, as wildlife is trafficked through our international airports and docks on its way to its final destination.

Ocean Invaders

Scientists predict an increase in invasive species in our waters over the coming years. Many of these will become integrated, and cause localised extinctions of native species. Within our seas, researchers estimate that over the coming decades the colonisation of invasive species could result in irreversible structural damage to planktonic, pelagic

SEAFOOD FRAUD

You could be a victim of wildlife crime without even knowing it. Seafood fraud – the mislabelling of seafood products – is becoming increasingly commonplace. As seafood is one of the most lucrative commodities traded globally, and with dwindling stocks of popular species, the incentive to label one species as another is appealing to sellers. The global supply chain for seafood is complex, and with most fish processing taking place at sea on enormous processing ships, away from the prying eyes of fisheries observers, it's easy to carry out the mislabelling. In a recent 2021 study by the *Guardian*, one in three restaurants across Europe sold mislabelled seafood. Sadly it can be hard for consumers to detect, as many species are indistinguishable from the labelled product once they have been processed. If possible, purchase seafood products from a local fishmonger where you can identify the fish prior to it being prepared. They will always happily prepare it for cooking for you and you'll be supporting local fishers too – win-win!

SHARK AND CHIPS?!

Research from the University of Exeter in 2019 has uncovered the grim reality of the fish in our nation's favourite dish. Ever wondered what 'rock', 'flake' or 'rock salmon' are at your local chippie? Fish and chip shops and fishmongers could be using these generic names to sell us endangered sharks under the disguise of our battered favourites. Scientists used DNA barcoding to identify species on sale and have found several shark species including starry smooth-hounds, blue sharks and nursehounds. There are nuances around the naming of food products, and this is not technically illegal.

It does, however, cause confusion for the consumer and indiscriminate names like these make it easy to commit seafood fraud. Would you willingly eat shark, an animal with a high concentration of dangerous metals in its meat, or if you knew it was an endangered species? The same research team also identified that the fins of endangered shark species like scalloped hammerheads, shortfin mako sharks and small-eye hammerhead sharks, are being sold by British wholesalers. Since this research, and as a result of a successful environmental NGO campaign, in 2021 the UK Government banned the import and export of shark fins.

and benthic communities. Not only will this have implications for the health of the biodiversity that lives in these ecosystems, but also for the commercial fisheries and aquacultural industries that depend upon them. Take jellyfish, for example. Across the North-east Atlantic we have observed an dramatic increase in jellyfish blooms. As these blooms encroach on UK seas, they could have enormous consequences for a number of sectors – predating fish populations, stinging unsuspecting recreational swimmers, and clogging up commercial fishing nets.

Invasive species can be extremely problematic for an ecosystem. They can alter the balance of native flora and fauna as they often outcompete native species for food and other resources such as shelter. Invasive species are also typically stronger than their indigenous counterparts, preying on or parasitising native species which are usually ill-equipped to fight back and have little to no defences. Invasive species are an enormous threat to wildlife worldwide and are frequently overlooked by the general public when considering the biodiversity crisis. It's important to remember that all ecosystems, especially those found on isolated islands, are highly specialised and an invasion of a non-native species can trigger a catastrophic domino effect that can lead to their complete restructuring. Some

scientists and conservationists consider the threat of invasive species to be even larger than that of the climate crisis. The subsequent economic fallout caused by invasive species can also have huge consequences for local communities. In 2021, an angler fishing off Chesil Beach in Dorset identified the first record of an invasive lionfish. This species has decimated native wildlife around the

WHAT ARE INVASIVE SPECIES?

We class invasive species, such as the Chinese Mitten Crab below, as those that are introduced and cause harm to an environment beyond their native range due to human activity. Their presence within an ecosystem usually threatens the native biodiversity as they have not evolved alongside non-natives and are unable to complete with them for resources.

▶ **Native species** are indigenous within an ecosystem via natural processes rather than human intervention.
▶ **Non-native species** or **introduced species** are also distributed outside of their native range as a result of human activity. This could be via an intentional introduction or accidental because of the transportation of species to a new region through shipping or on marine debris . Non-native or introduced species are not necessarily invasive as they may exist cohesively with other species without posing a threat to indigenous species.

Gulf of Mexico and the Caribbean Sea, so its newly found presence in the UK is extremely worrying. It is not yet clear why they are here or whether it was a fluke, but one theory is that with warming waters as a result of climate change invasive species like lionfish will have an easier time establishing themselves in our traditionally cooler waters.

Once they have become established within an ecosystem, invasive species can be tricky to eradicate, and it can take considerable time and resources to manage them effectively, if at all. It is much easier, and cheaper, to introduce preventative measures for alien species on ships and in fishing gear to reduce the risk of an introduction than to remove them once they've become successfully established within an ecosystem.

No More Fish for the Table?

Although climate change will become more pressing in the future, overfishing is the biggest threat to the ocean today. Decades of overexploitation have started to catch up with us and the saying 'there's plenty more fish in the sea' no longer applies. Exploiting our seas faster than the rate at which they can re-populate themselves threatens not only the food and economic security of those that depend upon them, but also the wider functionality of their marine food webs and ecosystems. A 2021 report by Oceana identified that of the top 10 most economically important fish stocks in the UK, six are overfished. It's clear that we need to do something about how we approach fishing, but unfortunately – as with many areas of conservation – there is no one-size-fits-all approach.

Worldwide, our population increases by approximately 80 million people per year, and with that seafood consumption rises by roughly 1.5 percent a year, putting more and more pressure on our ocean. Seafood is one of the most expensive commodities traded globally, so it's a lucrative business. And as standards of living around the world improve and more people can afford seafood, it is likely that our ocean will be put under even greater pressure. In the Western world our tastebuds are largely conditioned to salmon, tuna, cod, sea bass and prawns, which puts intense pressure on these populations to keep

THE PACIFIC OYSTER

Introduced by fish farmers for aquaculture, the Pacific oyster is a non-native species that has become prolific in the UK. These bivalves are particularly prevalent in southern England's coastal waters. Devon and Cornwall have seen huge population increases. Unlike those of native European oysters, the biogenic reefs formed by Pacific oysters smother intertidal gravels and mudflats, making it challenging for birds and young fish to forage.

up with demand. Here in the UK, we export the majority of what our fishing fleet catches, and the majority of what UK consumers enjoy is imported. Over 90 percent of cod consumed in the UK is imported from Iceland, Norway and Russia, whereas 70 percent of UK-caught seafood is exported to Europe and Asia. Since leaving the EU this difference in taste has become increasingly apparent with fish merchants experiencing difficulties in sourcing the fish preferred by the UK, and wholesalers experiencing difficulties in exporting fish from UK waters. Diversification of our seafood menus is desperately needed.

Fishing is a complicated business, and its complexity

is often overlooked by the public. As an island nation, the culture of fishing is intimately woven into our heritage. It is considered a fundamental part of delivering our food security, while also notoriously one of the most dangerous professions in the world. We have a romanticised image of the fishing industry and a profound respect for the fishers who make it all possible. But the fishing industry can also be deeply problematic for our ocean and its sustainability. Fishing fleets globally are much more than the small-scale fishers that we may first imagine. They also comprise enormous industrial-scale ships with nets the length of football fields (above) – termed 'supertrawlers' – that drag up everything in their path along the seabed. These enormous supertrawlers operate along our coastline and have even been observed fishing within Marine Protected Areas. They are more than just fishing vessels;

they are factories at sea. Factory ships, as the name suggests, enable commercial fisheries to catch, process and pack seafood at sea, improving efficiency from source to plate. These vessels often spend weeks, even months, at sea. Through the capture of unintended species (bycatch), such as including cetaceans, sharks and even seabirds, this destructive method of fishing devastates life in our seas for the sake of a handful of commercially valuable species. Wrapping your head around the monumental impact the fishing sector can have on the ocean is a challenge in itself. How *did* we get to this point?

In recent decades the fishing industry, like much of society, has been revolutionised by technology. As we moved from man-powered and steam-powered fishing vessels at the beginning of the twentieth century to diesel- and petrol-powered boats around the mid-twentieth century, fishers could spend more time at sea and travel further to find fish. This was accompanied by revolutions in fishing gear technology and the development of hardware such as fish finders and sonar technology that assisted fishers in their quest to hunt more fish.

Commercial fishing has become intensified and industrialised with such precision that we can suck life from the ocean like a vacuum, and yet the technology is not advanced enough to distinguish between a target and non-target species.

Between 30 and 40 percent of UK fish stocks are currently overfished. The capacity to catch fish is increasing and demand is growing too, but the number of fish left in the sea to catch is decreasing dramatically.

Gear type is important too when considering a fishery's sustainability. Some fishing methods can be highly damaging to the marine environment, such as dredging, which acts like a rake, scouring life and sediment on the seafloor, and accelerating the rate life can be removed from our ocean. Another example, bottom trawling, is one of the most destructive fishing methods in existence. Here, humongous heavy nets are dragged across the seabed, devastating everything in their path. As the ocean continues to be emptied of fish, fishers are going deeper into its depths in search of prized species. Nets may be dragged along the ocean floor a quarter of a mile or more beneath the surface, reaching previously pristine habitats. Scientists also think that fishing gear that drags along the seabed is unlocking stored carbon too, fast-tracking the release of greenhouse gases in our atmosphere and with it, climate change. A recent 2020 study by the Marine Conservation Society found that bottom trawling still takes place inside 98 percent of UK offshore Marine Protected Areas. If this happened on land, there would be public outcry. When it happens in our seas, we can't see the mass destruction of our precious marine habitats that it causes.

CATCHING MORE THAN OUR DINNER

Species caught unintentionally by fishers and discarded or landed (depending on local laws) are termed 'bycatch'. The Food and Agricultural Organisation defines bycatch as 'the unintentional capture of marine species while catching certain target species'. Bycatch can include different species (including seabirds), undersized or juvenile individuals of a target fish species, or it may be the other sex of a species fishers intended to catch. Fishers sometimes discard bycatch while it is still alive, but the trauma of the catching and releasing process typically still results in death. Not all fisheries are the same, however. Whether bycatch is likely to survive is highly influenced by which fishing gear caught it. Fishing methods like longlining and gillnetting can generate vast amounts of bycatch, and for many species it is one of the biggest threats to their future. Worldwide, scientists estimate up to 320,000 seabirds are killed annually in longline fisheries alone.

KEY CONCEPTS

Fully fished: When fishing pressure on fish stock is at the maximum limit of what we deem sustainable before overfishing occurs.

Overfishing: This is the act of fishing an area so much that it depletes the population of fish beyond the limit we deem sustainable.

Out of sight, out of mind.

Fishing isn't a problem, but at an unsustainable rate and using damaging gear are. So, what exactly is 'overfishing'? Defined in the *Oxford English Dictionary*, to overfish is to 'deplete the stock of fish by excessive fishing'. Between 2001 and 2020 the UK fishing fleet reportedly landed 1.78 million tonnes of fish more than what scientists considered to be the sustainable level. Not listening to the science can have devastating consequences for the future of our fisheries and the livelihoods that depend on them. Many of the world's poorest countries and most vulnerable communities , not to mention our marine wildlife, depend on seafood as their primary source of protein and essential nutrients, and so we must ensure that fish stocks are exploited at a sustainable rate.

Fishing Down the Food Web

Humanity has depleted the world's fish stocks to such a point that fishers are now required to fish for longer in order to catch sufficient fish to make their trips worthwhile. In doing so they are using more expansive nets that increase the risk of overexploiting target fish populations and the amount of bycatch.

The concept that we are fishing down the food web was first presented in 1998 by renowned fisheries scientist Daniel Pauly and has become one of the most cited fisheries science papers in history. It's not just another theoretical scientific concept either; at sites across the world we are seeing it play out in real time.

The Firth of Clyde in western Scotland, for example, was once home to a plentiful herring fishery. It was one of the most productive in Europe, providing the backbone of the local fishing community. Despite a ban on bottom trawling as early as the 1800s, the intensification of Scottish fishing practices resulted in fish stocks starting to show signs of depletion by the mid-twentieth century. Whilst intuitively, fishing restrictions should have been strengthened to allow the herring stocks to recover; instead, the bottom trawling ban was lifted in the 1960s, allowing the exploitation of bottom-dwelling species like haddock and cod. Over time the bottom-dwelling and mid-water populations collapsed and could no longer support a viable fishery. As a result, fishers transitioned to targeting crustaceans like scampi and scallops, but this type of fishing required heavy gear that created enormous devastation on the seabed. Today, 98 percent of the commercial fishing catch in the Firth of Clyde is made up of invertebrates. It is a textbook example of fishing down the food web in practice, and of the seemingly irreversible consequences intensive commercial fishing can have on an ecosystem.

Making Fishy Decisions

As you may imagine, because of the enormous complexity of the fishing industry and its role within society, it is also a hot political issue. In recent years this has been crystal clear as we have watched the departure of the UK from the EU. Now that the UK has left the EU, we have also left the Common Fisheries Policy, which was the guiding framework for fisheries management across Europe. The waters of the UK had been governed alongside those of the EU since 1972, but it is now an independent

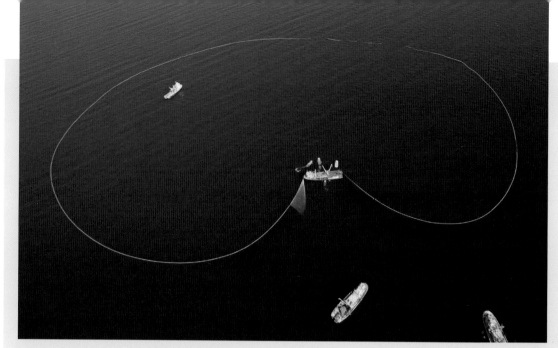

Purse seine

TYPES OF FISHING METHODS

▶ **Gillnets:** A gillnet acts as a long wall or curtain of netting that drifts in the water column and works by ensnaring fish by their gills. They are either anchored to the seafloor or attached to buoys to keep them from sinking. The size of the holes in the net (mesh) can be altered to target different sized fish but this does not stop bycatch.

▶ **Demersal or bottom trawl:** Trawling involves capturing a large number of fish by towing a big net along the seafloor behind a boat, or sometimes two. This method of fishing is popular worldwide due to its efficiency and ability to fish to deep depths, but it is also an indiscriminate method so involves high numbers of bycatch as well.

▶ **Longlines:** Longline fisheries involve a long fishing line fitted with baited hooks trailing behind a boat, sometimes for fifty kilometres or more. There may be 15,000 hooks on a single long line. Sharks and seabirds are frequently caught in pelagic longliners as bycatch.

▶ **Purse seine:** Purse seine fishing works by encircling an entire school of fish – usually a species like tuna or mackerel – with a vertical net which acts like a curtain. The bottom of this

Dredges

net is then closed like tightening purse strings. Bycatch of species like dolphins and seabirds can be high in purse seine fisheries.

▶ **Pots and traps:** Pots or traps aim to target crustaceans like lobsters or crabs and are usually made from materials like wood, wire, or plastic. Fishers typically bait them and deploy them on the seabed for 24 hours before hauling them aboard to harvest the catch.

▶ **Pelagic or midwater trawls:** Similar to bottom trawls, pelagic and midwater trawls work by towing a large net behind a boat. They differ from bottom trawls as they are designed to target fish in the surface and midwaters, like herring and mackerel. Bycatch is also typically high for these fisheries.

▶ **Dredges:** Dredges are composed of a bar which is like a rake that drags along the seabed to harvest scallops, oysters and clams. It works by dislodging the shellfish from the sediment and collecting them in a basket behind the frame. As a result dredges can cause substantial damage to fragile seabed habitats.

Demersal or bottom trawl

coastal state, so this is a huge change. In the new age of UK fisheries management, it is hoped that sustainability will be at the heart of marine policy, creating a prosperous future for fishers and providing the ocean with the chance it needs to recover from our activities.

Within the UK, fisheries management involves a number of different governing bodies, including the Department for Environmental and Rural Affairs (Defra), the Centre for Environment, Fisheries and Aquaculture Science (Cefas), the Marine Management Organisation (MMO) and 10 Inshore Fisheries and Conservation Authorities (IFCAs), each with their own district. There are many moving parts, and it can be difficult to keep tabs on who is responsible for the monitoring, management and enforcement of each element. Managing incredibly stretched

OVERFISHING ISN'T ONLY ABOUT FISH

Overfishing doesn't only have consequences for fish stocks and human food security; it also has catastrophic consequences for other marine life. For example, cod and sandeel stocks are vital for delivering global food security and for supporting marine species within different food webs. Overexploitation of sand eels in the UK has hugely impacted seabird populations like puffins, which rely on them as their primary food source. Puffins have had to supplement their diets with pipefish, which are less nutritious and cannot be adequately digested by their chicks. Twinned with exploitation from the fishing industry is a shift in the range of the sand eel's prey – a type of plankton – which is also causing a reduction in their populations. Ocean ecosystems are intimately tied to each other, and it is increasingly clear how vulnerable they are to humanity's impact.

resources, along with our departure from the EU, fisheries management bodies are under strain, yet they are vital to delivering the rigorous environmental protection needed by our precious marine environment.

Of course, it's not just our ocean suffering from a period of continued depletion. This is a human catastrophe too. For example, small-scale local fishers using traditional methods are often outcompeted by industrial fishers with technologically advanced gear and engine power. Smaller fishers are usually located in poor communities and find it hard to make enough money, and the number of fishers in the UK has halved in the last 20 years. On top of this, fisheries managers must navigate the threats of illegal, unreported and unregulated (IUU) fishing as well as the ever-present threat of seafood fraud – the mislabelling of seafood, usually in order to bypass laws and regulations surrounding restricted species or landing requirements (the rules surrounding the amount of and species of fish that are allowed to be bought to land from the sea). With so many varying factors, people's livelihoods at stake and a perishing marine environment, achieving

FUNDING THE FISHING INDUSTRY

The fishing industry is a costly business. Needing to pay for everything from gear maintenance to fuel bills, investing in the latest technology and competitively pricing a catch – not forgetting paying staff too – the fishers themselves more than often make a loss. Governments of the world supply funds, often sourced from taxpayer money, subsidising their commercial fishing fleets to allow them to continue fishing. It's not uncommon for fishers to earn more through subsidies than they do by catching fish. Subsidies are also highly controversial as they have been used to buy rights from developing nations to fish in their waters, such as off the coast of western Africa, which has had devastating impacts on local communities, economies and food security.

sustainable fisheries policy and management is a monumental mountain to climb, but is equally one of the most necessary objectives of our lifetimes.

Fish Farming (Aquaculture)

Aquaculture, or the farming of marine animals and seaweeds, appears on the surface to be a fabulous idea. With a growing demand for seafood and the increasing destruction of wild fish stocks, it seems sensible to fast-track production. For this reason, the public generally overlooks the true impact of the aquacultural sector. Salmon farming is big business in Scotland where enormous netted pens (page 91) are located offshore to house the salmon as they grow, exposing them to natural environmental conditions. When we think of salmon farms in the tranquil lochs of Scotland, we do not envisage the culling of seals by farmers or salmon with rotting flesh, covered in sores and parasites. Instead, thanks

WHAT IS THE FISHERIES ACT?

Established in November 2020, the Fisheries Act enables the UK to control who fishes in its waters by requiring licenses for foreign vessels that wish to fish within the UK's 200-nautical-mile economic exclusion zone. The Act focuses on sustainability, with an aim to ensure healthy seas for future generations of fishers. It seeks to deliver new fishing opportunities through international negotiations, to drive economic growth for coastal communities around the country. It is the legal template for policymakers and stakeholders involved with fisheries management in the UK.

to clever marketing, we have an idealised image of the sector and think how wonderful it must be for the salmon to swim in their native home, albeit in a net, before the end of their days.

Despite its ecological and welfare impacts, Scottish farmed salmon is the UK's most valuable food export. It is rated third in the world behind Norway's and Chile's production, and provides immense benefits to local communities and the national economy. These are the complex conflicts that environmental managers and decision-makers must negotiate.

Atlantic salmon farming dominates the UK's

STEALING FROM THE SEA

Illegal, unreported and unregulated (IUU) fishing can occur anywhere within our global ocean. It can be carried out by small-scale fisheries and industrial-scale ships across the high seas and within each country's economic exclusion zone – sometimes it's even associated with organised crime, human trafficking and slavery. Researchers estimate that up to one-third of all landed fish globally was captured via IUU fishing methods – an estimated 26 million tonnes per year – with the associated damage caused by IUU fishing practices within the EU alone worth £1.1 billion. IUU fishing is a nightmare for fisheries managers and conservationists as it slows progress toward sustainability goals and can be problematic for fish stock assessments. It can also have enormous repercussions for the food security of vulnerable communities and undermines the livelihoods of honest fishers. IUU fishing may take place in Marine Protected Areas, where harmful fishing practices are prohibited, which jeopardises the success of the protected area. All it takes is one IUU fishing vessel to undo years of recovery.

aquacultural landscape, but it's not the only thriving aquaculture here. Another example is the farming of shellfish, such as mussels and oysters, which is a relatively environmentally friendly practice. Mussels are farmed offshore in Cornwall and Devon, with Brixham the most prominent site in England at over 15km², and the first in Europe to receive a Best Aquaculture Practice certification. The booming shellfish aquaculture sector is a promising solution to our increasing appetite for seafood and the environmental challenges we face. Shellfish is currently not as popular with the public as cod and haddock. Our demand for these familiar favourites drives the desire for commercial fishing vessels to exploit these populations at a rate beyond that of their natural ability to repopulate. Still, if we incorporated more farmed shellfish into our diet, as a substitute for our favourite wild-caught fish (which are overfished), we would lessen the impact on our seas.

It's not uncommon for species to be farmed for release into the natural environment to improve 'recruitment' into the population too. Recruitment within fisheries science refers to

the act of transitioning between two stages of life. It is how very young, small fish survive to become slightly older, larger fish. The National Lobster Hatchery in Cornwall leads the way with this and has released more than 100,000 juvenile lobsters back into the sea to date.

Aquaculture goes beyond bolstering food resources or improving populations, though. We cultivate around 700 species of seaweed on UK shores, with much of it destined for use in animal feed, fertiliser and even glass production. Yet seaweed is a nutrient-dense, low-carbon protein alternative growing in popularity. Could our plates be piled high with seaweed in the future instead of cod?

As our global ocean and wild fish populations undergo increased pressure from exploitation and a changing environment, there has been an urgent requirement to find more sustainable alternatives to fulfil our desire for plentiful seafood. Fish farming, also known as aquaculture, has been suggested as a solution to the problem of feeding people. In fact, aquaculture is the fastest-growing food sector on the planet – increasing by over 527 percent since 1990. However, aquaculture is not without

its problems, sadly. Issues with fish farming include escape risk, disease and eutrophication caused by their feed and waste. Farmed fish such as salmon are also fed on smaller wild-caught fish, defeating championed sustainability merits. While salmon production is most often associated with fish farming, with Scotland being a world leader, farming of shellfish such as oysters (left), scallops and mussels is thought to provide a net environmental benefit and could be the most sustainable seafood choice of all.

FISH WELFARE IN SALMON FARMS

Modern fish farms create a breeding ground for disease that can cause widespread suffering. The overcrowding of salmon within fish farming pens spawns infestations of parasitic sea lice. These lice feed on skin, mucous and blood-producing white 'death crowns' of exposed flesh on the salmon. In attempts to dislodge the lice, salmon jump up to 30cm into the air and skim along the water's surface with their tails, displaying distress and discomfort. Skin lesions, loss of scales and ultimately death are often results of sea lice infestations. Salmon farmers go to immense efforts to remove these infestations, yet the steps they take are also damaging. Lumpfish and wrasse have been harvested alive from the wild marine environment to curb salmon lice infestations as they naturally predate on these aquatic insects. This can have unintended consequences on wild populations of these fish without proper management or regulation. Chemicals are also used to remove the lice, and antibiotics are used to keep the fish healthy. These pollutants enter our oceans, water systems and our own bodies when we consume the fish, further supercharging antibiotic resistance. Overall, the intensification of salmon farming causes serious animal welfare issues, widespread habitat destruction and potential drug-resistant superbugs.

Mending a Collapsing World

It is impossible to have a healthy planet without a healthy ocean. And it is impossible to have a thriving society without a thriving planet. We have left our ocean battered and bruised after decades of unsustainable abuse in the interests of human development. At the time of writing, the 2021 United Nations Intergovernmental Panel on Climate Change (IPCC) report has confirmed ongoing changes to our ocean, including warming, more frequent marine heatwaves, acidification and reduced oxygen levels. This report states that 'many changes due to past and future greenhouse gas emissions are irreversible for centuries to millennia, especially changes in the ocean, ice sheets and global sea level rise'. In addition to this, our global ocean faces immense pressure from overexploitation of its riches, habitat destruction, the introduction of invasive species and the pollution of its pristine environments.

But what's done is done. We cannot turn back the clock. But we can move forward

into a new era of ocean conservation and management through a system that advocates for healthier seas for all life on Earth. Science shows that if we leave our seas alone to recover, they can bounce back from our onslaught. What is important now is that we acknowledge the errors of our past and move forward collectively to a progressive green future that follows the science.

4

Sustainable Seas

Modern ways of life threaten the very existence of the
wonders below the waves, even though our collective
survival depends on them. How do we reverse our past
mistakes and allow our marine life to thrive again?
Striving for sustainable seas is something we
should all actively be doing in our everyday
lives. The challenge that lies before
us is not straightforward, but we
must face it head-on.

Successfully managing our seas is met with an entirely different set of trials and tribulations to those we encounter during terrestrial conservation. Saltwater moves with the currents and tides, and so does much of its biodiversity. Yet pollution also drifts with the ocean gyres, and fishing vessels relocate in search of new stocks to exploit, making life even more difficult for conservationists and enforcement officers. The very dynamism that makes the ocean so biologically rich is also what makes it so challenging to manage and conserve. Wildlife does not recognise international boundaries.

Nothing in the ocean is uniform. Coastal areas, for example, are typically under more direct pressure than pelagic regions because of their proximity to human activity. At the same time, the industrial and highly unregulated manner in which fishing activities take place on the high seas is also a major cause for concern. Threats vary in intensity depending on their locality and the region in which they're taking place, meaning there is no one-size-fits-all approach to marine conservation and sustainable management. This can create a considerable headache for scientists, conservationists and decision-makers alike. When we consider ocean protection, it's not enough for us to focus only on the UK marine environment – we must consider, too, what is happening in neighbouring seas, how that directly affects UK waters and how our actions here impact others elsewhere. We must act locally and think globally.

It is not all doom and gloom. Our ocean is in a state of emergency, which is growing by the day, but there are plenty of reasons to be optimistic about the future too. Now it's time

WHAT DOES 'SUSTAINABILITY' MEAN?

Sustainability has become a trendy term that marketing managers and politicians like to throw around as the public becomes increasingly conscious of the impact of our actions on the planet. But what does sustainability truly mean? We define it as the rate of consumption that allows resources to replenish naturally rather than putting them in deficit. In the context of the ocean, it is possible to have sustainable fisheries if we do not take too many fish and leave a good population structure that allows young fish to mature and mature fish time to reproduce. But be careful about greenwashing – some organisations use the word 'sustainable' without any evidence that it applies to their actions or products. Often, 'greener' products are more expensive too, so it's in the brand's interests to portray this image so that they can charge us a higher price. With this in mind, it's always important to do some background research before investing in a new purchase.

historically been overlooked by Western scientists. Yet their knowledge and understanding of our natural world are invaluable, and we must incorporate their expertise into our plan for a flourishing world. Simply put, science is made better by diversity.

The urban and technologically advanced modern world's detachment from the natural environment and all that it does for us is also partly to blame for the predicament in which we find ourselves. When given the opportunity, young people are absorbed by the natural world, engrossed in its wild curiosities

for some ocean optimism. A wave of hope is growing mightier every day, and soon will become a tsunami of change. You, holding this very book right now, are a part of that brewing tsunami. Over recent years, the collective power we can wield has been demonstrated as we've embraced the plastic-free movement and more people have taken a stand against the climate emergency and ecological breakdown. Collaboration is key to a healthier future for our ocean. There is a place for all of us in the quest for a planet thriving with life again. People of every age group and from every background across society must unite for the common cause of diverting our global community from its current dispiriting path. Listening to diverse voices and experiences strengthens our understanding of the world. It empowers us to create robust solutions to the challenges facing our planet's global community, which can provide for everyone. Communities living on the front line of the climate crisis and ecological breakdown, such as those from indigenous groups, have

that feed their growing minds. Yet we are losing them, and ourselves, to an artificial world in which technology consumes our realities and social media can warp our sense of self. Forming a connection with nature early on in life is the key to forging a generational commitment to its betterment. It can also be vital to deepening our relationship with ourselves and the world around us by improving our mental health. For me, experiences at an early age

sparked a lifelong fascination with the sea, and working with young people has given me hope for the future. You may have similar childhood memories of spending time immersed in nature, whether inland or on the coast. We must continue to harness our innate desire to connect with the world around us to secure a greener – and bluer – future for our planet.

Looking ahead, we need to restructure the way society uses and values the ocean. The aspiration must be to conserve the marine environment so that it can thrive once again, while simultaneously using the ocean-derived resources that so many communities depend upon at a sustainable rate. We all need to think ocean. Change can be an uncomfortable thing to experience, no matter how necessary it is for the future. While ignoring the warning signs may be more comforting, scientific research shows that if we continue to do so, our planet will be something of an apocalyptic world by the end of the century. Short-term strain for long-term gain is a sacrifice we should be willing to make. It is no exaggeration to say that if our ocean dies, life as we know it will die

with it. So, what steps can we take to avoid this harrowing scenario?

Nature-based Solutions

What if we could work with nature, rather than against it? For millions of years on our planet, biodiversity has been working with physical and chemical processes to ensure an equilibrium that supports all life on Earth. But since the industrial revolution, we have disrupted this delicate dance between life forces by pumping ever-growing amounts of greenhouse gases into the atmosphere. Disrupting the balance of the system on which life depends is an obvious threat to life as we know it. But what if there was a solution right under our noses that could go a considerable way toward righting our wrongs?

Restoring our natural environment through nature-based solutions is the light at the end of the tunnel. As the name suggests, nature-based solutions use nature to combat the environmental obstacles we face. Climate change, water and food security,

KEY CONCEPTS

Coastal resilience: the ability of a coastal community to actively react to the impacts of natural disasters such as hurricanes and storms or severe flooding events at the time of the incident, rather than merely recover from the aftermath.

Blue carbon capture: the carbon captured by the world's oceans and coastal ecosystems.

SAVING SEAGRASS - REMEDIES

Across the UK, as you read this book today, scientists and conservationists are teaming up to rewild the nation's seagrass meadows. Pilot studies will help inform researchers on the best places to locate seagrass restoration projects alongside current human activities like boating and angling so that conservationists can maximise the benefits to society and life under the waves. With less than 1 percent seabed coverage, seagrass can deliver 10–18 percent of the ocean's total buried carbon storage. Despite being unseen by many of us, seagrass meadows are a vital tool in our arsenal as we seek to rewild our seas and combat climate change.

The LIFE Recreation ReMEDIES project, headed up by Natural England, is a perfect example of how we can manage a seagrass restoration project. By training volunteers, installing advanced mooring systems and cultivating up to 25,000 plants a year, this project aims to restore four hectares of seagrass meadows in the Plymouth Sound. Projects like this, which occur at a local level but deliver results globally, are vital to maximising our collective conservation efforts across the UK.

overdevelopment and severe weather events, like violent storms and flooding, are all pressures the global community must face as our population continues to grow and people seek a higher quality of life. Nature-based solutions can take many forms, from small-scale nature enhancement projects to innovatively restoring entire ecosystems. At their core, nature-based solutions offer ecosystem services – such as coastal resilience and blue-carbon capture and storage – that are crucial in the fight against climate change. By rewilding our lost habitats, we can reap the benefits of these natural climate-change mitigation strategies.

While nature-based solutions are widely documented on land, there is hope they can also be implemented for our marine environments. With our seas' immense carbon-storage potential, it would be foolish for us to overlook one of our greatest allies in the fight against these growing issues. As the UK works toward its target of net-zero greenhouse gas emissions by 2050, we must look beyond the boundaries of the land to the deepest depths of our home planet. Rewilding the seas will be a gargantuan task, but with colossal benefits for all of society.

Blue Carbon Heroes

The ocean has immense potential as a global carbon store and for maintaining biodiversity through ecosystems like saltmarsh, seagrass and kelp. Yet over recent decades, the UK has lost vast swathes of these climate-smart ecosystems – over 90 percent in some cases. So how do we restore these precious ecosystems to their former glory? Just as it's possible to replant forests, it's possible to re-seed their underwater equivalents. It sounds simple in theory, but habitat management at sea is never quite that easy! The ocean can be a precarious place, and as it is constantly in motion and under attack from damaging and illegal activities, it can be

challenging to maintain effective protection. However, once conservationists have identified appropriate areas for seeding and given those critical areas the level of management they required to recover, nature will take care of itself. And ultimately, nature will also take care of us in the process.

Coastal Forests: Rewilding our Saltmarshes

Saltmarshes (right) once blanketed the fringes of the Essex coastline. Yet over the last 20 years, more than 60 percent of them have been lost – mainly due to coastal development and sea-level rise. Saltmarshes are not only a vital source of blue carbon, but also play a considerable role in coastal defences, and they are important nursery grounds for species like the European sea bass, thin-lipped grey mullet and common goby. Along the Blackwater and Colne estuary, the Essex Wildlife Trust has been busy at work creating more than 70 hectares of new intertidal habitats. Using a coir structure – made of coconut fibres that are saltwater resistant – they have encouraged

the sediment accumulation and plant growth required to rewild saltmarsh habitats in the region. Five years on from its initial rewilding, the Fingringhoe Wick intertidal area supports a myriad of wading and wetland birds and provides an important fish nursery for species like the sand smelt.

Helping our Kelp

Kelp forests (top of page 100) are magical and those in Sussex were once a vast underwater world teeming with life. As recently as the 1980s, they stretched 25 miles along the West Sussex coast and were 2.5 miles wide. However, due to intensified trawling activity and dredging boats in the area dumping sediment, these majestic kelp forests have since dwindled to tiny remnants of their former glory. Now, thanks to the campaigning efforts of the local community, Sussex Wildlife Trust and Sussex IFCA, these mighty blue-carbon powerhouses have a chance to thrive again as damaging trawling activity is banned from an area of this coastline. The bid to revitalise Sussex's kelp forests is an example to us all that there is power in numbers and in using your voice to get traction for conservation action.

Operation Oyster

Oysters are the kidneys of our sea. They filter its water, cycle its nutrients and protect the coastline from erosion. European flat oysters once formed enormous biogenic reefs that blanketed the seafloor. It's estimated that we have lost over 90 percent of the native oyster beds in the UK. Today, several oyster restoration projects have made an immense effort to restore those oyster beds. The Yorkshire Wildlife Trust is doing exactly that within the Humber Estuary. Within 40 years, the substantial oyster beds of the Humber were wiped out by ongoing sewage pollution and the *Bonamia* parasite – a single-celled organism that causes lethal infections in shellfish. After working hard to improve the Humber's water quality and to ensure water pollution in the area would be reduced, restoration work began by reintroducing 3,000 European flat oysters to the estuary (right). Along with the necessary seabed restoration to build the foundations of an oyster bed, the reintroduction of oysters here is just the beginning. Over time, the project hopes to expand, with thousands more oysters.

Marine Protected Areas

If given a chance, our ocean can thrive once again. Establishing a Marine Protected Area (MPA) can offer marine life this chance. Marine Protected Areas are defined as geographical areas of the coastal or marine environment within which Government bodies such as Defra, the Marine Management Organisation (MMO) and the Joint Nature Conservation Committee (JNCC), typically restrict environmentally damaging activities. For example, certain types of fishing and sediment dredging cannot occur in areas with species or environmental features that are prone to damage and protected by national and international legislation. MPAs are a crucial weapon in our fight for a restored future for our seas and against the climate crisis, and are championed as a way of protecting precious marine habitats and wildlife across the globe. Scientific evidence of the benefits to society that MPAs can provide, such as replenished fish stocks and climate-change mitigation, is continually building. The positive results of MPAs often exceed our expectations.

It is hoped that these areas will collectively form a Marine Protected Area network that connects ocean habitats and allows migratory marine species to embark on their immense journeys to critical breeding and feeding grounds without interference from human activities. The UK's Marine Protected Areas will contribute to the 30 percent of the global ocean that science has called for to be protected by 2030. This goal is considered the minimum ocean protection requirement necessary to mitigate climate change and ecological breakdown. When choosing sites for MPAs, however, the established MPA network mustn't only protect more charismatic species, like grey seals, or commercially important species, like European sea bass, but must also protect often-overlooked elements of the marine environment. Sandy seabeds

and seaweeds are as important as deep-water corals and marine megafauna. In fact, marine habitats like muddy substrates are often highly biodiverse environments that are abundant with microfauna like marine invertebrates. We must preserve all our diverse ecosystems as much as we can.

Unfortunately, it's not enough to designate an area as protected and leave the ecosystem to get along with its recovery – although, in principle, this is all that's required of marine life. Around 98 percent of current offshore Marine Protected Areas are estimated to still allow damaging activities like bottom-trawling within them, for example. Marine managers and enforcement officers struggle to monitor and enforce protection of offshore sites due to their distance from shore. This makes it easy for IUU fishing to take place within them and

FLOURISHING MARINE LIFE IN NO-TAKE ZONES

The second no-take zone introduced in the UK and the only one designated by its local community, Lamlash Bay off the coast of the Isle of Arran in Scotland, is a sterling example of a community paving the way for ocean protection. Since 2008 the Bay has been off-limits from the commercial fishing industry and has been left to rewild. Scientists from the University of York and the Community of Arran Seabed Trust (COAST) partnership have been closely monitoring the site and have found signs of life flourishing. Scallop numbers have nearly quadrupled within the no-take zone alone, and these scallops are also much bigger than their non-protected counterparts. Life has returned to this area and continues to flourish year on year, with divers recently spotting a cuckoo ray at the site for the first time in 30 years. Lamlash Bay is a textbook example of how the ocean will repair itself and blossom once we give it the protection it deserves.

jeopardise the site's conservation. For marine protected areas to succeed, therefore, they must have sufficient funding for management, monitoring and enforcement from the Government to allow governing bodies like the Inshore Fisheries and Conservation Authorities (IFCAs) to safeguard these areas. With stretched Government budgets, this is never easy, particularly after the coronavirus pandemic. Arguably, however, there are few things more important to society than the prosperous future of our natural world, so it is in all our interests to ensure Marine Protected Areas do what they say on the tin: protect the marine environment.

One of the biggest obstacles to the establishment of Marine Protected Areas is the commercial fishing industry, which is understandably concerned that the livelihoods of British fishers will be impacted by restrictions on fishing activity. Yet, with dwindling fish stocks, fishers could find that Marine Protected Areas are the solution to securing their future. Research has demonstrated that MPAs can be effective beyond their boundaries with thriving wildlife inside the area spilling out into the surrounding (non-protected) sea. A 2021 study by the University of Plymouth indicated a 400 percent increase in fish present within the Marine Protected Area. Giving the ocean protection like this can provide signs of recovery within a few months, with staggering results after years of protection. It's like the ocean is releasing a big sigh of relief after being allowed to heal from humanity's continual onslaught, while also showing us the power of protection.

The term 'Marine Protected Area' has been used by the media and the public to describe a marine environment that has some form of protection. However, the levels of protection may differ slightly depending on an area's designation. It can all get a little bit confusing. In the UK, we have several types of MPA that provide varying levels of protection. Currently, only a handful of areas ban all extractive activities – these are called 'no-take zones'. Thankfully, however, this is all set to change soon. After environmental organisations, including the Wildlife Trusts, campaigned for the highest form of protection for our seas, the newly named Highly Protected Marine Areas (HPMAs) will be introduced from late 2022 onward and will provide a much-needed refuge for marine life from any damaging activities and disturbance. At the time of writing, almost all Marine Protected Areas within the UK allow some form of human activity within them. Conservationists and policymakers hope that HPMAs will protect the most vulnerable UK habitats and allow them to flourish again as marine wilderness areas where life can exist undisturbed by human activities. But what does marine protection currently look like within UK waters?

European Marine Sites

While it was a member of the EU, the UK introduced several European Marine Sites designed to protect wildlife and habitats that are important at a European level – these are known as Special Protection Areas (SPAs) and Special Areas of Conservation (SACs). At the time of writing, there are currently 116 SACs with marine components in the UK, 25 of which are within the UK's offshore waters such as the Pobie Bank Reef, off the Shetland Islands in the North Sea, and the Pisces Reef Complex, near the Isle of Man. There are also 123 SPA sites, including the Outer Thames Estuary in England and the Severn Estuary in Wales. You may come across sites with multiple designations, such as the Dogger Bank, which is an SAC and also a Marine Conservation Zone. Thankfully, European Marine Sites have been kept since the UK has left the European Union so these important marine habitats will continue to be protected.

KEY CONCEPTS

Marine Conservation Zone: an area that protects a range of nationally important, rare or threatened habitats and species.
Special Protection Area: an area designated for internationally important rare and vulnerable birds, which is important for their breeding, feeding, wintering or migration. These sites were designated under the Birds Directive (first iteration in 1979) by the EU.
Special Area of Conservation: an area designed to increase protection for biodiversity, which is deemed ecologically important at the European level as part of the effort to conserve biodiversity globally.

These sites are designated under the European Union's Habitats Directive (1992).
Area of Outstanding Natural Beauty: areas we protect via the Countryside Rights of Way Act (2000) to conserve and enhance the landscapes' natural beauty.
Site of Special Scientific Interest: an area of particular interest to science that is designated due to the presence of rare species of fauna or flora.
Highly Protected Marine Area: an area of the sea designated for protecting and recovering marine ecosystems. Extractive, destructive and depositional uses are prohibited, allowing only non-damaging levels of activities to the extent permitted by international law.

Marine Conservation Zones

In England, the most common form of Marine Protected Areas are Marine Conservation Zones (MCZs). These areas are designated to protect habitat and species deemed to be nationally important based on criteria generated by the JNCC or other international frameworks like OSPAR (the Convention for the Protection of the Marine Environment of the North-east Atlantic). MCZs have been in place since 2013, and the network has been expanding ever since, with more than 90 MCZs now in English waters.

MCZs can also be designated within Welsh and Northern Irish territorial and offshore waters too. Scotland has Marine Protected Areas rather than Marine Conservation Zones. These are some of England's notable MCZs.

THE BLACKWATER, CROUCH, ROACH AND COLNE ESTUARIES

As the largest tidal river in Essex, the River Blackwater is home to a mosaic of subtidal sediment habitats from sand to gravel to mud. They may seem lifeless, but these habitats

Colne Estuary

SUCCESS STORY: LYME BAY REEFS

If you need proof that Marine Protected Areas work, look no further than the Lyme Bay Reefs in south-west England. After years of campaign work by environmental organisations and the local community, the Government protected Lyme Bay from the damaging effects of dredging and bottom trawling. In 2011, the site was designated as a Special Area of Conservation, giving it further protection. Despite scientists predicting it may take up to 20 years for the area to recover, within two years, researchers identified that there were already signs that recovery was taking place. Lyme Bay Reefs feature spectacular diversity, with more than 300 species calling the area home, including nationally important species like the gorgeous pink sea fan and the mesmerising sunset cup coral (right). Thanks to the protections provided to the area, this exceptionally fragile underwater community can thrive again

now that we are protecting it from harmful heavy scallop dredges. Studies of the site by university researchers have also shown that the benefits of these protections go beyond the environment too, with local anglers, divers and commercial potters experiencing improved experiences and higher incomes.

along with those in the neighbouring Crouch, Roach and Colne estuaries, are home to important estuarine species. They protect the rare native oyster, an important biogenic reef-building species that provides a key habitat for other species like blue mussels and Ross worms. The Blackwater Estuary is an important site for the tiny lagoon sea slug, and is the only place you can find this endearing creature in the south of England.

Blackwater Estuary

WHY PROTECT THE SEABED

Much of our coastal and offshore seafloor is covered in thick sediment made up of mud, sand, silt, gravel, or a combination of all these elements. It may seem like this gloopy substance is barren of life, but it's quite the opposite. Despite often being hundreds of metres from the ocean's surface, marine sediments are dynamic environments. The seafloor shifts and changes over thousands of years as dead marine animals and phytoplankton sink and decompose into the sediment. This amalgamation of nutrients supports an incredible diversity of marine life, providing homes for marine invertebrates which in turn provide food for larger marine predators. What's more, the seabed also locks up huge amounts of carbon that has been absorbed into the ocean from the atmosphere, so the seabed is a helpful natural ally in the fight against climate change. By protecting enormous swathes of seabed from damaging activities through Marine Protected Areas, and Highly Protected Marine Areas (HPMAs), we can prevent this carbon store from being damaged and stop carbon from re-entering the atmosphere to accelerate climate change further.

MEDWAY ESTUARY
Featuring an eclectic mixture of estuarine habitats, the Medway Estuary between Gillingham and Sheerness in Kent is the residence of the tentacled lagoon worm, which bears resemblance to a creature from a science-fiction movie. This dynamic estuary supports diverse communities within its varied habitats and provides rich nursery grounds for many fish, including skate and sea trout. Mudflats, sheltered gravel areas and saltmarsh islands support the lives of many molluscs, worms and crustaceans that reside within the dynamic sediment. You can also spot seals as they bask in the sunshine on the estuary banks and a variety of wading birds as they search for food within the muddy sediment.

RUNSWICK BAY
Located to the north-west of Whitby, Runswick Bay MCZ is home to a highly productive seabed with a diverse range of habitats. From lush kelp forests to deep seafloors carpeted with sea sponges, sea squirts and starfish, there is an abundance of life within its waters. It's also an important spawning and nursery ground for many economically important fish like herring, cod, whiting and plaice. You can explore

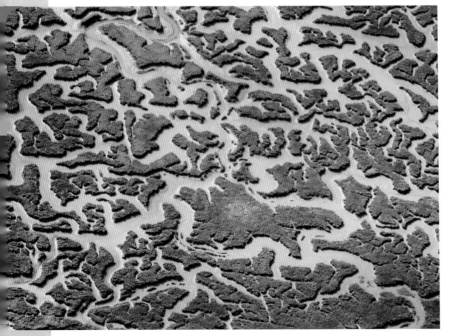

Medway Estuary

Runswick Bay MCZ at low tide as its shoreline is decorated with plentiful rockpools where you can spot blennies and butterfish. Make sure you keep your eyes on the horizon, as harbour porpoises and seabirds like kittiwakes are regularly spotted here.

FULMAR

More than 200km off the Northumberland coast there is an oceanic gem brimming with marine wonders. The Fulmar MCZ is a jewel in the UK's MPA network crown. As one of the deepest MCZs in the North Sea, Fulmar is filled with life of all sizes across its 50–100m depth.

Burrowing anemone (Fulmar)

Its muddy bottom is an important habitat for sea pens, ocean quahogs and burrowing anemones. Giving protection to its muddy and sandy seafloor enables an abundance of bivalves, worms and sea urchins to thrive, which support species higher up the food chain like seabirds and cetaceans. Fulmar is a spectacular location to see foraging seabirds on and over the water, from agile guillemots to impressive Arctic skuas, and of course the site's namesake, the stunning fulmar. Take a peek below the surface and you may also catch a glimpse of alien-like deep-sea shrimp and fabulous undulate rays, camouflaged against the mixed sediment seafloor.

HOLDERNESS INSHORE

With its rugged dramatic landscape, the Holderness coastline in East Yorkshire is a sight to behold. Beneath the surface is no different. Its seabed is home to a mosaic of habitats, from cobbly shores to mixed sediment, sand, peat and clay, supporting a wealth of diversity. An abundance of invertebrates live here, from turfs of hydroids and bryozoans, to reefs covered in Ross worms and even eight different types of crab! With

Common lobster (Holderness)

its alluring crimson and blush tones, the common sunstar is one starfish not to be missed. Bigger species like tope and smoothhound sharks and even friendly giants like the minke whale can be spotted from shore passing through the area.

LUNDY

Lundy Island is a national marine national treasure, and is most famous for its playful grey seal colony. Located in the Bristol Channel, Lundy Island is the location of some of the most spectacular marine life in the UK, thanks to its location at the meeting point of northern cold currents and southern warm ones. This meeting attracts a spectacular array of marine life that thrives on its immense biological productivity. Since 1986 Lundy has been a Marine Nature Reserve (one of only three in the UK designated by the Government to protect marine areas of national significance) and is a true testament to the success of nature's recovery if we afford it the proper protections. More than 300 species of seaweed can be found blanketing its reefs and rocky inshore habitats, whilst under the waves an intricate network of anemones, sea fans and corals provide a spectacular array of colour. You can even find the chocolate finger sponge thriving here. Lundy is also a birdwatcher's paradise, with Manx shearwaters, guillemots and razorbills crossing the sky and down to the rich waters to feed.

ALLONBY BAY

Sprawling along the Cumbrian coastline, Allonby Bay may appear to be lifeless, but the region is bustling with diverse invertebrates. From reef-building honeycomb worms to the charmingly-named baked bean sea squirt, numerous seaweeds and the bizarre-looking breadcrumb sponge, the list goes on! This MCZ features some of the best examples of biogenic reef in the north-west of England, so it's vital that we protect it for future generations to enjoy.

KINGMERE

Kingmere is a treasure trove of rock and chalk habitats famous for its breeding black sea bream. It's one of the most important regional locations for this fish in the UK. Black sea

Grey seal (Lundy)

bream are stunning fish with a familial instinct to protect their young as they build nests on the hard bedrock and accessorise them with sand and gravel. Thanks to the abundance of rocky habitats at this location there are plenty of nooks and crannies for marine life to seek shelter from predators and the prevailing currents. Along Kingmere Rocks you will find glorious fan worms flowing in the current, much as flowers sway in the wind. But that's not all this area has to offer. Worthing Lumps showcases the best underwater chalk cliffs in Sussex, and thanks to its protected status they can thrive for many generations to come. The cliffs are carpeted with life. A matrix of hydroids, tube worms, sponges and bryozoans cover the cliff face, and larger species like catsharks, spider crabs and tompot blennies take cover in the many rock cavities.

Tackling the Plastic Tide

Plastic is an enormous problem facing our seas. The UK Government has begun banning single-use plastics like straws and introducing a 10p charge for single-use plastic bags, with more bans on substances like microbeads and other single-use plastics like cutlery coming in over the next few years.

Kingmere

But much of the change that is required to make a sizeable dent in reducing our plastic consumption must take place within industry. British Airways, for example, are introducing several changes across their fleet such as removing plastic packaging from their inflight headphones, which will result in 45 tonnes of plastic being saved per annum. These are simple steps that make substantial differences, and as consumers we must continue lobbying big corporations to make these changes for our planet. On a personal level, there are also many steps that we can take to reduce our single-use plastic consumption. But other than banning and reducing our use of plastics, what actions can the Government take to reduce the nation's craving for plastic?

Deposit-return Schemes

Introducing a deposit-return scheme to the UK would reduce marine pollution and allow us as a society to place more value on the materials we use every day. It would also lead us toward a circular economy, whereby materials aren't lost but are recycled to be used again and again. A deposit-return scheme works by charging an additional small fee as a deposit when someone purchases a single-use item, like a plastic water bottle. This small deposit is refunded to the purchaser when they return the used item to a recycling point. These schemes have already been implemented in many other countries including Denmark, Germany and the Netherlands, where recycling rates of these materials are now above 90 percent.

Weren't Microbeads Banned in the UK?

After years of campaigning by environmental groups, in early 2018 the Government introduced a ban on the manufacturing of products containing plastic microbeads (tiny particles less than 1mm wide). A few months later, a further ban on selling rinse-off products containing plastic microbeads came into force in the UK, covering products like toothpaste and scrubs.

While this may sound like a great leap forward, it leaves many loopholes. The main problem is that plastic microbeads are still allowed in many other products, including

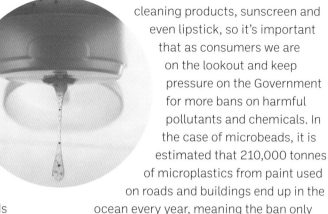

cleaning products, sunscreen and even lipstick, so it's important that as consumers we are on the lookout and keep pressure on the Government for more bans on harmful pollutants and chemicals. In the case of microbeads, it is estimated that 210,000 tonnes of microplastics from paint used on roads and buildings end up in the ocean every year, meaning the ban only influences a tiny part of the problem.

Menacing Microfibres

Each and every time we wash our clothes, millions of tiny synthetic microfibres (top of page 112) wash away into our rivers and

FAST AND FURIOUS FASHION

Fast fashion is an environmental and social-justice nightmare. Our obsession with bulk buying the latest styles and the growing popularity of revealing 'shopping hauls' on social media have contributed to a surge in fashion waste. Globally, the fashion industry accounts for 10 percent of carbon emissions and almost 20 percent of wastewater. It takes 1,800 gallons of water to grow the

cotton required to make one pair of jeans. An enormous amount of finite resources are needed to produce garments. Many workers within the industry experience injustices as they are underpaid and overworked in horrendous conditions. Many manufacturers now make clothes out of cheap, synthetic materials that contribute to the plastic crisis when they reach the end of their lives.

Our craving for fast fashion pollutes the marine environment, puts even more strain on finite resources, pumps greenhouse gases into the atmosphere during production and has dire consequences for human rights across the globe. It's up to all of us to curb our fashion addiction and source clothes responsibly whenever we can. Where possible, you can make a difference by only purchasing clothes when you need them, patching up holes in worn items and shopping from second-hand clothing stores.

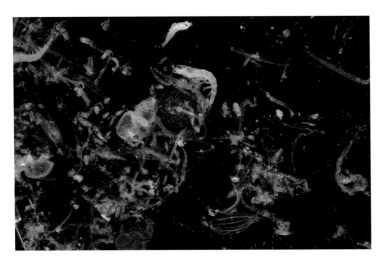

Sustainable Fisheries

Seafood is a critical part of millions of people's diets. Our seas must be sustainably harvested, not only for the future of marine life and the ocean itself, but also for the longevity of the fishing industry and all those who depend on it. Continuing to exploit our fisheries with a 'business as usual' approach is unsustainable and will further decimate marine habitats and drive species to extinction. In fact, in 2021 the second global assessment of sharks and rays established that overfishing is the leading cause of shark and ray declines globally, with habitat loss and climate change being secondary drivers. Meeting our demand for seafood has had devastating consequences for life in our ocean. Altering how we fish is ultimately one of the most important things we can do for the marine environment.

Moving away from fisheries management that only considers the impact on the target

coastal environments. At the last assessment in 2021, the Marine Conservation Society estimated that the UK polluted the environment with a whopping 9.4 trillion microfibres a year. A simple fix would be for the UK Government to introduce legislation that requires washing machine manufacturers to install microfibre filters in all new domestic and commercial machines. This would reduce the flow of microfibres into our ocean and other water courses at the source. They would operate in a similar way to lint filters within tumble dryers and would capture any fibres before they have a chance to make their way to the sea.

species to an ecosystem-based approach is vital for the sustainability of the sector. Essentially this means considering the impacts on the entire ecosystem when making management decisions – like how many fish we should catch and what fishing gear should be allowed in certain areas. Given how intimately connected every single element of the ocean is, this seems like a logical approach to managing fisheries. However, for decades we have put commerce at the heart of fisheries management, over the needs of the wider environment. If we protect fish nursery grounds and designate important habitats as no-take zones, we will give our marine ecosystems the chance to recover, and plentiful fish stocks will return. Ultimately, this will allow for higher landings and a more profitable and reliable fishing industry. Rebuilding and maintaining healthy fish stocks should be at the heart of a productive and profitable fisheries sector. Conservationists share a common cause with the fishing industry and it's crucial we do not lose sight of that.

THE WILDLIFE TRUSTS' SUSTAINABLE VISION FOR THE FUTURE OF UK FISHERIES

▶ Fish stocks restored to their maximum potential and then sustainably fished, allowing stocks to thrive
▶ Integration of ecosystem-based fisheries and marine conservation management
▶ Aquaculture that is integrated with planning and that has its impacts assessed at an ecosystem level
▶ Improved consumer access to local, sustainably caught fish
▶ Good trade conditions for fish and fish products
▶ Support and promotion of low-impact, sustainable fishing methods

Commercial fishing also remains a considerable threat to the health of our seas through its fishing practices, despite technological innovation and a deeper understanding of the destructive nature of certain equipment. In order to transition away from harmful practices like dredging and bottom trawling, the Government must also provide support for low-impact sustainable fishing methods, such as static gear like pots and traps, to improve their profitability. Through educating the public on the importance of choosing sustainably caught fish and creating good trade conditions for the sector, the viability of these methods should improve, making them more appealing to fishers. A healthy future for the fishing industry relies on a healthy future for our seas, and so it's imperative we work together to achieve this common goal for our oceans.

Marine Planning

It's clear that managing the marine environment is a tricky business. Not only is the ocean a dynamic place, constantly shifting and changing with the currents and other environmental pressures, but it is also heavily used by people. Given all the difficulties, how can the elements required for a sustainable union between the seas and humanity be brought together?

Enter marine spatial planning. This is a process used to ensure that the distribution of human activities within an area, such as fishing and tourism, are managed in a way that enables the achievement of ecological, economic and social objectives. By creating regional marine plans for our seas, we can meet the needs of the people who depend on these areas and the wildlife that live there without causing being detrimental to either.

For our ocean to be sustainably used, we must go beyond protecting it and implement sustainable management measures. Our society has a strong relationship with the sea, so conserving our ocean also involves working with people. In recent years the importance of marine social sciences – the study of the relationship between people and the sea, through psychology, economics, sustainable development and governance – has come to light. Through studying our relationship with the sea and understanding how different communities value and connect with the ocean, decision-makers and marine managers can ensure conservation measures balance the needs of the local people with those of marine life. This approach to protecting the ocean means engaging with the public so that the behavioural changes needed for conservation can be introduced. Marine social science can also lead to better stakeholder engagement and co-management of Marine Protected Areas within a coastal community, ultimately making them more successful.

We can achieve our international commitments to environmental sustainability. We can ensure equal access for all users of the marine environment in a way that has the least-damaging impact. We can allow our seas to prosper once again with a network of well-managed Marine Protected Areas. None of this is beyond the realms of possibility. It will take collaboration across all of society to ensure everyone's voices are heard. It will require innovation and bravery as we seek to manage our marine environment in a way that has never been adopted before. But ultimately, it will allow us to have a sustainable relationship with our seas for the future.

Paving the Way for Sustainable Seas

Rewilding our seas sounds like a daunting task. But it's also exciting to imagine our seas teeming with life again as though they were untouched by human activity. Across the UK

HOW MUCH IS TOO MUCH?

When it comes to fisheries, you probably often hear the term 'quotas'. But what is a quota? Put simply, it is a share of a fishery's catch or fishing effort allocated to an individual fisher. Typically, specific quotas for specific species are part of a fish stock's total population. For a fishery to be sustainable, scientists calculate the Total Allowable Catch (TAC) each season for applicable species and allocate a proportion of this to each fisher with rights to the quota. The quota is either catch-based (the amount of fish caught) or effort-based (time spent fishing) fishing. As fisheries are devolved within the UK, the quota method used will depend on different factors, such as the country where the fishery is based.

In the UK, only five companies control almost a third of UK fishing quotas, and just 25 companies control more than two-thirds. Typically this means less money trickles down to local economies than with small-scale traditional fishers. Larger companies often also use less sustainable methods.

we have evidence of communities coming together to campaign for the protection of our precious coastline, and winning. Current Marine Protected Areas demonstrate that if we limit damaging activities, or stop them entirely, life underwater will rebuild. We know that nature can be our biggest ally in the battle against climate change, and we also know that rewilding will be paramount as we seek to reverse ecological breakdown and habitat loss.

Sustainability is the buzzword of our generation – and for good reason. For us to achieve true sustainability, we must completely re-invent how we approach management and conservation of the marine environment, but critically, we must listen to the science. On the international stage, the UK is committed to a range of international biodiversity and climate targets, such as the United Nations Sustainable Development Goal 14, which aims to improve life in the ocean and our sustainable use of its resources by 2030. The UK is a key player in the global movement for 30 percent of the ocean to be protected by 2030 through its commitment to establishing a blue belt of

more than 4 million km² of Marine Protected Areas across its overseas territories. These changes at a national and international scale are imperative if we are going to stand a chance in the battle against an increasingly warming planet and the growing ecological crisis. These changes must no longer be political talking points, but political action points. As the blue economy develops, it must operate with sustainability at its heart. We are running out of time. But if we act now, we can divert our ocean from the calamitous future it currently faces.

But what must we as individuals do? As global citizens there are many actions that we can take every day that can have a hugely positive impact on our seas, and in some cases even spark big businesses and governments to take note too. We must never underestimate the power we have as individuals and as communities when we use our voices to try and turn the tide. As a collective, we can create enormous waves of change. The next chapter describes the many steps you can easily take to become an ocean warrior. Let's get started.

CHAPTER

5

Be an Everyday Marine Conservationist

We all want to do our bit for the beautiful blue and be ocean heroes. It's time for some ocean optimism so let's take action for the big blue in our everyday lives, knowing even small changes can turn the tide.

The next few years will be critical for the planet, and we have the power to make sure the road we take is the right one. This ocean revolution must take place across all facets of society, with governments and international corporations leading the way to create a vibrant blue economy that works for people and the planet. Most importantly, ocean recovery must be at its heart. Transformation at a governmental and industrial level is paramount, but there are many things you can do to secure a better future for our global ocean. Never underestimate your power to change the world for the better.

You may feel like your impact is insignificant, but when we all combine forces through small daily actions, they quickly add up. The ocean is vast, but so is our impact upon it. By adopting climate-friendly habits, you can begin to turn the tide. Whether you're an established eco-warrior or a concerned global citizen, this chapter has something for you. Be the change you want to see in the world. The following list is by no means exhaustive but is a fin-tastic starting point for anyone interested in becoming an ocean defender.

Battle the Climate Crisis

All life on Earth is connected. Every action you can take to battle the climate crisis will ultimately benefit life in our oceans. Due to the time lag between the carbon we pump into our atmosphere today and its impact on our ocean, by cutting our carbon now we can reduce the future consequences for our ocean. There are numerous ways you can cut your emissions, from flying less frequently to walking more or taking an active role in your local community and championing climate issues with your government. We can all be climate champions.

Switch Up Your Diet

Dietary choices are a hot topic. No one likes being told what they can and can't eat. Cultures are built around food, and we derive much pleasure and social value from sharing a meal with family or friends. Yet industrial-scale animal agriculture has been established as a leading cause of greenhouse gas emissions and land-use change, with experts estimating its contribution is at least 15 percent of global annual emissions. Clearly, we need to rethink our relationship with food and its production. You can significantly reduce your carbon footprint by cutting meat from your diet, but if you're not ready to make the commitment of removing meat entirely you can still make a difference simply by consuming less meat and introducing more sustainably sourced seafood into your diet.

Vegetarianism and veganism have surged in popularity over the last decade. With more meat-free alternatives available it's becoming easier, and cheaper, to try eating a more plant-based diet. Even if you don't want to avoid meat entirely, switching to a vegetarian or vegan meal once a week could, according to a 2019 study, cut UK greenhouse gas emissions by 8.4 percent. You can have great fun in the kitchen learning new recipes that avoid animal products!

Remember, though, that not all vegetarian and vegan foods are created equal. For example, increased demand for avocados has led to deforestation in Central and South America, pressure on finite water resources, and social injustices, such as food insecurity, for the farmers that produce them. It's a lot to consider, but we must be smart with our money and food purchases, and, if you can, it's often worth doing a bit of extra background research. When shopping look for foods with fewer food miles and produced with organic farming methods, which are far kinder to our planet and not always as expensive as we think.

Go Dairy-free

Nowadays cows' milk is not the only available milk product on the market, with a whole range of plant-based alternatives out there. From almond to rice, oat to soya, there's one for every set of tastebuds. Plant-based milk alternatives are recognised as better for the environment than cows' milk, but again they are not all created equal. Increasing evidence indicates certain plant-based options have their own negative social and environmental impacts, with, for example, almond milk requiring vast amounts of water to produce. Taking into account both land and water use along with greenhouse gas emissions, oat milk is now widely considered to be the most environmentally friendly option, so try to introduce that into your diet where possible, for example with breakfast cereal, in baking or a hot drink. Cows' milk has a far higher environmental impact than plant-based alternatives, but if you do opt for cows' milk, consider registering for your local milk round where available, as it is delivered in reusable and recyclable bottles, avoiding the plastic waste associated with milk bought in supermarkets. Around 4 percent of the British population are signed up to a delivery, and momentum is growing, so why not try it out?

Buy Energy-efficient

It's becoming easier for consumers to purchase electrical appliances that are energy efficient as they become cheaper and more readily available. Electrical appliances in the UK are rated from G (least efficient) to A (most efficient)(above), making it simple for you to make an informed choice. Energy-efficient electricals are often more cost-effective, too, saving you precious pennies and making your home more eco-friendly in the process. Don't forget to turn off and unplug any electricals you aren't using.

Sustainable Spending

Your money has the power to change the world. Ethical banking is a fast-growing sector as consumers try to avoid investments that favour fossil fuel companies. Many of the UK's most popular banks are leading investors in fossil fuel companies and other environmentally damaging industries like deep-sea mining and mineral extraction. Where you choose to invest your money is influential. By banking with an ethical bank, such as Triodos and the Co-operative Bank, you can support investments into green technologies (bottom of page 121) and socially responsible projects that are working to make the world a better place, rather than maintaining business as usual.

Cut the Flying

If you fly frequently, is there another way to get from A to B? Travelling across the UK by train (below) is more scenic and much better for the environment. We all love exploring new places and cultures, but have you considered holidaying in the UK and sightseeing on your front doorstep (check out Chapter 6 for some ideas). Limiting the number of trips you take abroad each year can do wonders for your carbon footprint. For example, a return flight from London to New York can contribute almost a quarter of an average person's annual greenhouse gas emissions. As a result of changing consumer attitudes, the aviation industry is investing significantly into reducing its carbon and plastic footprints through greener fuels and reduced wastage. You have the power to create change on a transnational scale just through where you choose to spend your time and money.

Offset Your Carbon

If you do travel by air, you can offset the carbon emissions created by your travel plans. Many airlines offer the opportunity to offset your carbon emissions by making a small financial contribution that is then invested in projects that reduce our collective carbon footprint, like restoring forests (right) or planting seagrass seeds. Offsetting carbon has been criticised as a method of greenwashing; however some experts have argued that whilst it will not tackle climate change alone, voluntary carbon offsetting can fund habitat restoration projects or climate smart technologies like green energy that can buy us time and progress the solutions needed to halt the climate crisis. In addition to offsetting your carbon, you can also look out for products that are registered as being carbon neutral. Certified B Corps companies, that put people and the planet at the heart of their business, are a good starting point for your search.

Plastic is Not So Fantastic

We love the ease of single-use items, and in some cases they save our lives. Without single-use personal protective equipment (PPE), our fight against the coronavirus pandemic would have been much harder and medical procedures in hospitals across the globe would be impossible. However, as a society, we have come to depend on single-use plastics far more than is necessary. Plastic objects infiltrate every aspect of our lives, and once we've used them, they spend the rest of their days plaguing our environment and suffocating wildlife (below). We must stop making so much plastic stuff and prevent it from getting into the ocean. Reducing your plastic consumption is a tangible action you can take for cleaner seas. Once you start ridding your life of plastic, you may quickly realise how many unnecessary plastic products you use by

sheer habit. Making sustainable swaps can also save you money too. As a consumer, the power really is in your hands – big businesses depend on your money to drive their production, so you can create change on a big scale by making a statement with your cash.

Bring Your Own Bottle

For many people, a significant way to cut plastic waste is by investing in a reusable water bottle. It's estimated that every day in the UK, an average of 35.8 million plastic bottles are used, but only 19.8 million are recycled. Also, it is often cheaper for our Government to ship our plastic waste overseas, which burdens communities without the necessary infrastructure to recycle it properly. Plastic bottles are also one of the most frequently found items on beaches worldwide, and their lids commonly end up in seabirds' stomachs. The plastic ring that keeps the top attached to the bottle also commonly entangles and suffocates marine life. If all of us switched to a reusable water bottle, we would go a long way to minimising the impact of single-use plastic on our planet.

No More Plastic Bags

As a result of the UK Government introducing a 10p levy for single-use plastic bags, demand for them in England dropped by 59 percent in a year. Simple initiatives like this can have huge impacts. Worldwide, the picture is very different,

and it's estimated that 500 billion plastic bags are used annually. Every time you leave for the shops, remember to bring an eco-friendly bag with you. Whether you choose to use a jute or canvas tote or shopper bag, they can be used time and again to help reduce your impact on our planet. A 2011 UK Government report estimated that a new cotton bag must be used 173 times to be more eco-friendly than a plastic bag, so try not to accumulate more of them than you need. Alternatively, upcycling clothes such as an old pair of jeans to make your own cotton bag is an even more eco-friendly option.

Straws Suck

Businesses across the UK have now ditched the plastic straw because of a Government ban. As consumers, we must continue to use straws only when necessary and, if we're able, we should use alternatives such as bamboo, glass, aluminium and paper instead. Plastic

Scrap the Cling Wrap

Cling wrap cannot be recycled and can end up in our ocean after floating down rivers or being blown off landfill sites. Once in the ocean, sea turtles may mistake it for their favourite food, jellyfish, as it looks very similar when drifting in the current. Consider using aluminium foil, biodegradable wax paper bags, reusable eco-friendly stretchy lids or beeswax wraps when you need to wrap sandwiches or cover leftovers. You can find many alternative styles on the market, with beeswax wraps in particular coming in many attractive designs. Beeswax wraps are typically made from eco-

straws can take up to 200 years to decompose and may end up littering our seas, where they can choke marine life. A heart-wrenching viral video that showed a sea turtle with a plastic straw stuck in its nostril played a part in convincing people around the world to reduce their plastic usage.

Remember that not everyone is able to remove plastic straws from their lives; some people depend on them for medical reasons or to facilitate independent living. It's vital we don't demonise people for what they can and can't do and acknowledge that there are many other ways to join the ocean-friendly movement.

Tweak Your Caffeine Fix

Roughly 2.5 billion disposable coffee cups are thrown away every year in the UK. Most of these contain unrecyclable materials and can spend up to 50 years degrading in a landfill, if they break down at all. Shops and supermarkets are filled with affordable and trendy reusable coffee cup options, made from eco-friendly materials like bamboo and recycled plastic. Less than 1 percent of the 2.5 billion coffee cups thrown away every year in the UK are recyclable, so by making the switch, you can make a massive reduction to your plastic impact.

friendly materials, such as pine resin, cotton and local beeswax, so you don't need to worry about any chemicals leaching into your food. Other options like aluminium foil and paper bags are more budget-friendly conventional options that are easy to adopt and don't cost the Earth.

Spork It!

To avoid using plastic knives and forks when you're eating outdoors, carry some reusable cutlery with you when you're out and about.

By using a reusable spork, bringing your own from home or opting for compostable alternatives like bamboo, you could personally save 466 items of unnecessary plastic every year. The UK Government announced in 2021 that it plans to ban single-use plastic cutlery – hopefully single-use cutlery will be a thing of the past.

Choose a Corker

We've become reliant on the convenience of the plastic-coated screw-top wine bottle, but popping a cork is undoubtedly way more satisfying. Next time you head out for a bottle of wine, if you can, choose a bottle with a natural cork stopper instead of a screw cap. Many of these caps also contain BPA, an industrial chemical used to make certain plastics, further damaging the environment and potentially human health, whereas cork is natural and derived from the cork oak tree, so it biodegrades after use. Natural corks are made from the bark of cork trees. So they are natural and biodegradable. Cork is also renewable and sustainable, and harvesting it, doesn't harm cork trees. Cork trees can live for as long as 300 years and each time their bark regenerates itself, it absorbs CO_2 in

the process. Don't worry though if you're unable to make this switch – there are many reasons, including physical conditions, that you may not be able to pull a cork, and there are plenty of other ways to be ocean positive.

FINE TO FLUSH
Certification mark*

Don't Feed the Fatberg

Wet wipes have become another huge environmental problem triggered by consumer behaviour. Many wet wipes are comprised of plastic particles, which make them robust and almost impossible to break down. Unfortunately, many people have picked up the habit of flushing wet wipes when they're finished with them. From here they enter the sewage system where they accumulate and do not break down. Not all of us can avoid wet wipes all the time. On occasion they can feel essential, whether we might need them for childcare or to refresh ourselves after a long, hot day outside whilst camping or at sea. Choose biodegradable (or, better still, reusable) wipes when you know you don't have to flush them after use. And for any wet wipes that you know you will need to flush away, make sure they're *Fine to Flush* standard, which indicates that the wet wipes can be safely flushed down toilets. This certification ensures that these wipes meet the criteria necessary to break down within our sewer system and don't cause nasty sewer blockages or fatbergs – a mass formed from fat, grease and wet wipes washed down the drain, which clogs sewers.

Give Up Smoking

Smoking cigarettes is not only terrible for your health, but the remnants after they've been used are one of the most prevalent forms of marine litter. Cigarettes contain single-use plastic filters that, according to the Marine

Conservation Society, are regularly within the top five items found on UK beach cleans. It is thought that single-use filters and cigarette butts can take roughly 14 years to degrade within the marine environment. As they do this, they release chemicals and microplastics that pollute their surroundings and are ingested by marine life. If you choose to smoke, please dispose of your cigarette butts properly.

Plastic-free Period

During their reproductive lifetimes, women in the UK are estimated to use 11,000 disposable menstrual products. Tampons, pads and panty liners typically contain considerable amounts of single-use plastic and other synthetic materials that can accumulate within our environment if not disposed of properly. It was recently estimated, for example, that a single pad may be up to 90 percent plastic. In an average year, this totals 200,000 tonnes of waste entering UK landfills, which can take centuries to degrade. One of the simplest ways we can reduce our environmental impact is by switching to reusable or eco-friendly period products such as a menstrual cup, cotton tampons

in paper packaging or washable pads. You can find these alternatives online or in the supermarket, with many stores now stocking a range of options.

Review Your Brew

Did you know that the teabags from some tea brands are riddled with plastics? Yes, that means with every cuppa we're drinking a delicious concoction of microplastics too. Yummy. Or not. According to a 2019 study, one plastic teabag releases around 11.6 billion microplastics into one cup. How about making the switch to loose-leaf tea or a plastic-free teabag instead? A quick internet search can pull up a long list of brands that have ditched the plastic. As a rough guide for the supermarket, watch out for tea brands that use polypropylene, a sealing plastic, to keep the teabag from falling apart – these are neither recyclable nor compostable. If you prefer to carry on drinking microplastics, make sure you dispose of your teabags properly afterwards to ensure the plastics they contain don't enter our waterways. Composting is a great way to dispose of teabags, but there is debate on whether this is moving the plastic problem from one environment to another. Depending on how much tea you drink this could mount up.

Stop Chewing Plastic

Did you know that chewing gum contains plastics? Here in the United Kingdom, we are the second-biggest consumer of chewing gum globally, chowing down on a rough average of 130 pieces every year. Chewing gum contains plasticising substances, which are bad for you and the environment too if not disposed of properly. If you're guilty of chewing gum – and I am too – there's an emerging market for plastic-free gum, so you can easily make the swap today.

Glitter: Once It Arrives, It Never Leaves!

Many of us love a bit of sparkle, whether at home or a summer festival. It can easily find its way into the ocean by trickling down our drains, and then enters our food chain when plankton and shellfish ingest it. In essence, glitter is essentially tiny plastic particles that are lethal to life in our oceans, and is hard to dispose of responsibly as it falls off outfits, decorations and faces. As a result of consumer demand, eco-friendly biodegradable glitters are increasingly becoming the norm, with more and more brands and colours available online. Enjoy some guilt-free glitz by purchasing responsible glitter for your next party.

Keep Plastics Away

Limit the number of plastics you bring with you to the beach. Despite our best intentions, little pieces of plastic can slip out of bags or pockets and drift across the beach, especially on windy days. Reusable water bottles, bags, straws and utensils should make up your beach lunch kit. Make sure you clear any rubbish when you leave, and why not do a quick two-minute beach clean while you're at it too? Leaving only footprints and the beach in a better state will ensure that it is an enjoyable environment for everyone in the future.

Conscious Consumption

Plastic often takes centre stage in discussions about conscious consumer choices for the environment, but many damaging chemicals and materials are lurking in our cupboards that we should try to avoid. It can seem hopeless at times – we have so many other things to think about in our busy modern lives. Our capitalist consumer culture is built upon ease of purchase for this reason, and eco-conscious options go against that – they can take considerable time to produce and can be hard to identify. When you're worried about other things in your life, like caring for family members, paying the bills and work commitments, it can be a struggle to remember to consider your impacts on the environment too. But the more we, as consumers, choose to apply pressure on industries to think about the environment and change their products and practices for the better, the greater the range and availability of eco-conscious options we'll have, making it a little easier for us to do the right thing by our planet.

Watch What You Wash Away

We are inundated with chemicals across every aspect of our lives. From cosmetics to cleaning

REDUCE YOUR RUNOFF

Fresh water is a finite resource. There is a limited amount of water on our planet, so we should ensure we're responsible water users and conserve as much as possible. Here are some tips for how you can save water:

▶ Take shorter showers
▶ Turn the water off while brushing your teeth
▶ Only use your washing machine when you have a full load; consider hand washing garments when you only have small amounts of washing to do
▶ Use a water butt to collect rainwater to use in your garden
▶ Turn off automatic watering systems in your garden when it rains

products to soaps, we cannot escape them. Many of these have toxic impacts, not only on our wildlife but also on our health. Before washing chemical waste down the drain, check the bottle to see that it is not poisonous or hazardous. Our drains are often connected to rivers and streams, which eventually end up in the ocean. For this reason, we should not underestimate the influence our household wastewater can have. If unsure, you can always go to a waste refuse site to dispose of the substance properly. Facilities to dispose of substances like paint, cooking oil and car fluids are commonly available.

Ditch Dirty Dishes

Invest in eco-friendly washing-up liquid and cleaning sprays to reduce your chemical runoff into our waterways and oceans. Wildlife-friendly brands to look out for include Ecover, Method and Bio-D, and some supermarket brands have also cut out the rubbish from their products and changed to natural eco-friendly ingredients. Not only are these products better

for the environment, but they're also often better for you, as they're less harsh on the skin and have a minimal impact on the air quality in your home. You can also do your bit by purchasing cleaning products with less plastic packaging.

Wash for Wildlife

You can have a positive impact on our planet just by making some changes to the way you wash your clothes. According to a 2020 analysis by Which?, simply by washing clothes at 30 degrees instead of 40 you can make a 38% energy saving and cut your carbon emissions. If you can, avoid using the tumble dryer as much as possible and instead opt to air-dry your washing on a line or a clotheshorse around your house. As with other cleaning products, you can choose eco-friendly and biodegradable laundry detergents, which are better for the planet and less harmful to life in our rivers and seas. Try to wash your clothes only when they're dirty rather than after one wear – your bills will thank you too!

Forget Fast Fashion

The fashion industry is one of the most significant contributors globally to climate change. Many of the clothes we wear are created using synthetic plastic microfibres, which account for 35 percent of the microplastics found in the environment. Fish and shellfish mistake these fibres for food, and they enter the food chain, eventually making their way up to us. The worst culprits for microfibre shedding are clothes made from polyester fleece, nylon and polyester fabrics, so check the label and avoid buying these if you can. Although more expensive, if you can afford to, consider investing in clothes made from close to 100 percent natural materials, like cotton. Not only are these materials better for the environment, but your clothes will also last longer.

Use Ocean-safe Sun Cream

Sun cream is a necessity on a hot summer day to protect our skin from harmful ultraviolet rays. Yet the very substance designed to protect our skin is having detrimental impacts on life under the waves. Many sun creams on the market include chemicals that contain nanoparticles that have devastating consequences for marine creatures, from deteriorating reefs to changing the sex of fish. The key ingredient to avoid is oxybenzone and to instead choose a mineral-based sun cream that uses zinc oxide or titanium dioxide. Ocean-safe sun creams, while more expensive, are increasing in availability and often last longer too. Wearing a hat and UV-protective clothing can also reduce the amount of sun cream you need by up to 90 percent, so remember to cover up and protect your skin, and the planet, when you're out in the sun.

Be an Ocean-friendly Pet Owner

Just like us, our pets need feeding, and we can make ocean-friendly dietary choices for our animal friends. You can follow similar seafood sustainability guidelines for your pets as you do for yourself. Also remember not to flush cat litter down the toilet and if you have a dog, dispose of its faeces properly in the designated bins as animal faeces contain harmful bacteria that can be dangerous to aquatic life. If you keep fish, remember to never release any from your aquarium into the wild. This introduction of non-native species can have catastrophic impacts on native ecosystems and species if they establish themselves.

Fish Are Friends, But Also Food

Tackling overfishing is one of the biggest obstacles to a healthy future for our seas and the wildlife that lives there. Millions of people across the globe depend on seafood for critical nutrients in their diets. In fact, if harnessed correctly, a landmark scientific study published in 2021 has revealed that food derived from the ocean, termed a 'blue food system', could feed the world sustainably and deliver the nutritional needs humans require to thrive better than any other food group. Yet not all fishing methods are equal, with some having monumental consequences for our seas. Small-scale fishers using sustainable fishing gear are much more ocean-friendly than enormous supertrawlers with fishing nets the length of football pitches, for example. As a consumer, it can be tricky to navigate all this information. How do you decipher what seafood you should be consuming, particularly in a world fraught with seafood fraud? How can you make the best choice for the ocean? How do you know what you should eat and what you shouldn't? You will never get it 100 percent right, but there are steps you can take to sustainably source your seafood.

Avoid the Red List

How do you know what seafood you should be avoiding? You can easily identify what fruits of the sea you should be eating and which you should run a mile from by following the traffic-light system in the Marine Conservation Society's *Good Fish Guide*. Avoid red-rated species as they're typically endangered, overfished, caught through destructive fishing methods or caught illegally. Green options should be your go-to as they're non-threatened species that are fished sustainably using the least environmentally damaging methods. This wonderful all-encompassing guide is free to use and readily available on the Marine Conservation Society's website and as an app. Even better, the list is frequently updated too.

Check for Eco-labels

There are a range of eco-labels that you can search for to identify the sustainability of your seafood. Not all eco-labels are founded equally – each has its own criteria for selection and some drawbacks – but some consumer guidance is definitely better than nothing. The Marine Stewardship Council (MSC) blue tick is the most well-

known. You can usually find products with their approval stocked in all major supermarkets. Whilst the MSC accreditation is not without criticism, opting for this over no certification is the better choice. Their sister organisation, the Aquaculture Stewardship Council (ASC), now also certifies the sustainability of farmed seafood such as salmon and shellfish.

Spending Wisely for Sustainable Seas

Different types of fishing have different levels of impact on our ocean, so it's essential that we keep this in mind when purchasing our seafood. Some methods dredge heavy nets across the seabed, causing catastrophic damage to fragile ecosystems. In contrast, other methods like rod and line fishing are highly selective and take one fish at a time, reducing bycatch to almost nothing. Always ask at the counter when buying your seafood, or check the packet, to avoid destructive methods with high bycatch like dredging, longlining and bottom trawling. For ease, you can look it up in the *Good Fish Guide*, which includes this information in its traffic-light rating.

Mix It Up

If you eat seafood, you will probably be consuming cod, haddock, salmon, tuna or prawns. They may be delicious, but when our demand for these five species is high, we put considerable pressure on the ocean. Alongside this, here in the UK, we export two-thirds of what our local fishers catch because the species caught in our waters don't suit our current palates. It can be daunting trying a new species for the first time, but there's

lots of advice online on how to cook each one. Highly sustainably bivalves like farmed oysters and mussels are a fantastic place to start and a low-carbon option too. If shellfish isn't your thing, why not head to your local fishmonger and try their catch of the day? Handline-caught mackerel, Dover sole, Cornish hake and red gurnard are excellent choices. Maybe you'll encounter a new favourite, and it's a great way to support your local fishers. However, 'local' doesn't always mean 'sustainable', so it's still important to look out for the status of a fish on eco-guides and eco-labels.

Fish Responsibly

Fishing for fun can be a great way to engage with the marine environment and get youngsters interested in life below the waves, forging a lifelong relationship with the sea. When doing so it's key to fish responsibly and ensure you're complying with local laws, regulations, and best-practice handling guidelines. Catch-and-release angling is increasingly popular, and if you're looking for fish for supper there are few methods more sustainable than catching fish yourself! Just make sure you're complying with minimum landing sizes, which you can find on your local

Inshore Fisheries and Conservation Authorities (IFCAs) website and return safely to the sea anything you don't wish to keep so that it can continue to grow and maintain the population.

Out and About

Everyone loves being in the great outdoors and spending time by the ocean. But how do we make sure we're having the least impact? It's surprising, but even when we feel as though we're being as conscious as possible about our surroundings, we can still have a negative influence by disturbing wildlife. Forging a connection with our natural world is key to a lifelong desire to protect it, but how do we do so responsibly?

Make the Connection

Spending time in, on or by the sea is a marvellous thing. It is one of life's greatest pleasures, and the feeling of being surrounded by saltwater is something that keeps people returning to the big blue time and time again.

We feel relaxed by it and are in a constant state of wonderment as coastal and marine species spark our imaginations. The earlier in life that we can create this connection, the better. Once this relationship has been established, it's important to further our understanding of the natural world and our connection to it. Beyond your experiences of the coast, you can continue learning every day about things you can do to help protect and restore the seas through books, documentaries and online articles. Even if you live hours away from the coast you can champion its conservation with your everyday actions too. Sharing the information you've learned and tips and tricks you've mastered to protect our seas with friends and family is a great way of expanding ocean optimism, and inspiring others with your love for life in our ocean. Why not help spark their fascination for the ocean by offering your book recommendations or watching your favourite documentary with them? Bring your loved ones into the ocean movement.

Practice Safe Boating

Spending time on the water is an immersive way to connect with our ocean. Feeling the salt spray on your skin, smelling the all-too-familiar fishy smells of the seaside, and watching the waves lap against the shore are a delight to the senses. When boating, watch out for where you anchor as it can be destructive to fragile habitats like reefs and seagrass beds. If you can, anchor away from these delicate ecosystems and use sandy areas instead. Practice safe boating by adhering to 'no-wake' zones and minimising disturbance caused to sea life by following the Wildlife Trusts codes of conduct (available on their website) and maintaining a respectable distance.

others to join in next time! It's worth checking in with your local Wildlife Trust, too, to make sure you're following any necessary health and safety regulations.

Organise a Beach Clean-up

Want to do more for your favourite marine patch? Why not get some friends together and organise a beach clean? Beach cleans are the perfect way of engaging the local community in marine conservation issues and inspiring people to practice daily changes in their lives that will help our seas. Ideally, identify a day with great weather to maximise the turnout and pick a location where there aren't regular beach cleans to boost your impact. Harness the power of social media to advertise your beach clean and take lots of photos to encourage

Travel Responsibly

We all love to travel and experience the thrill of experiencing new places, encountering adventures around every corner, and learning about the beauty of the world around us – after all, we weren't born to stand still. When you're travelling, be aware of your impact on the environment and make sustainable decisions so that future travellers can enjoy your favourite sites. If you join an ecotour, choose a responsible operator that puts the animals' welfare ahead of profit. By looking

on review websites you can easily identify any red flags from other tourists be guided by sustainable tourism certifications. Remember to support ecotourism operators that support the local economy, rather than transnational corporations that do not trickle money down to local communities. Sustainable and responsible tourism is possible, but in order to make it the norm we must work in tandem with people and the planet.

Observe the Code of Conduct During Wildlife Encounters

Beautiful basking sharks, dancing dolphins and smiley seals are all sights any wildlife lover would be overjoyed to see during a trip to the coast. If you're lucky enough to encounter one of our impressive marine animals while in or on the sea, follow the voluntary code of conduct on interactions to minimise disturbance, which differ depending on the species. Make sure you never chase an animal, and, if it comes to you (as above), maintain a respectful distance as much as possible. Overstaying your welcome or getting too close to any animal can result

in a fight-or-flight response, leading to energy losses, less-effective feeding, fatigue and a reduction in reproductive success. You can find the code of conduct on the Wildlife Trusts website. Stick to the code and remember, no touching!

HOW CAN I BE A SUSTAINABLE OCEAN TRAVELLER?

▶ Respect marine animals and their wild spaces
▶ Take photos and selfies at a safe distance away from animals
▶ Clean up after yourself when visiting beaches and natural spaces
▶ Before travelling, research the region's local seafood and fishing practices to help you make sustainable food choices.
▶ Once you're there, ask locals for advice and look for sustainable seafood certifications in restaurants.
▶ Partake in eco-tourism activities that support local communities

Leave Only Footprints and Take Away Only Memories

It can be tempting on a trip to the beach or on faraway adventures to take a piece of the ocean home with you. Sadly, however, many familiar and popular seaside souvenirs are often harvested in unsustainable ways, which has a detrimental impact on local wildlife populations. When we consider everyone's individual actions together, even taking a few shells and a small bottle of sand can greatly influence the entire ecosystem's health. In fact, in the UK under the Coastal Protection Act 1949 it is illegal to remove any natural material like sand and pebbles from public beaches. So, next time you visit the seaside, don't take home souvenirs like dried seahorses, coral jewellery, tortoiseshell hair accessories or shark teeth. Leave only footprints and take only memories.

Take it to the Next Level

So, what's next? You've followed the advice offered in this chapter, from simple swaps to fighting climate change and taking action on the coast by cleaning beaches and respecting wildlife. You've become a fully fledged ocean protector, but now you want to do more. It's time to take all you've learnt to the next level

and influence change in your community to bring more people on board with the ocean movement.

Think Ocean in the Workplace

You don't need to be a marine scientist to save our seas. Whether you work in business, construction, or teaching, you can rally ocean support from your organisation and contribute your skills to the marine conservation movement. There is a place for all of us in the quest for a circular blue economy that prioritises ocean recovery and the wider planet. You can use your unique skill set to make a difference – we need all hands on deck!

Take a Political Stand

Power to the people has been proven to work time and time again, with public support for the plastic-free movement triggering businesses and the Government to initiate change as a result. So what's next? Join the global fight for more protection for our seas by backing the 30 percent of the ocean protected by 2030 pledge. Take a stand against local and national issues that affect our coasts and rally community support behind them. Write to your MP about conservation issues you are passionate about and encourage the Government to take a stand. Keep up to

date with the latest ocean policy by regularly checking the news and following ocean-friendly organisations on social media. Boost the campaign work of the Wildlife Trusts, too, as they fight for a wild future for our seas. There are many worthwhile campaigns to get behind for ocean recovery – pick one which resonates with you and take a stand.

Speak Out for Sustainable Seafood

Consider only spending your money with companies committed to serving sustainable seafood. Raise concerns when you see unsustainable seafood being offered in restaurants and supermarkets, especially if you spot a threatened species on the menu or at the seafood counter. Share evidence on social media to raise your voice for marine life and respectfully garner public pressure for the outlet to make a change. Don't forget to commend businesses when they are committed to sustainable seafood.

Be an Online Ocean Advocate

Never underestimate the power of social media. Thanks to the global reach of online social platforms, you can have a huge impact with just a little bit of effort. By publicly adding your voice to marine conservation campaigns, you can encourage your friends, family and other people online to take note and consider supporting them. Always make sure you do your research – spreading misinformation can be detrimental to conservation and just as dangerous as having no information on a topic. We live in an era of so-called 'fake news', so always read up as much as you can, and don't be afraid of speaking out.

Educate Yourself

With 95 percent of our oceans remaining to be explored, there are still many mysteries for scientists to uncover. There is always more to learn about our marine environment, which

makes this saltwater journey you are on even more exciting. Continuing to learn about life below the waves will empower you to educate and inspire more ocean defenders to join the movement for our living seas.

Be Part of Our Ocean's Future

Connecting young people with our coast early on in their lives is an easy way to improve the odds that they'll be committed ocean protectors for life. Whether it's a trip to the seaside for rockpooling or a day at the beach to enjoy the sun, you can encourage the young people in your life to forge a strong connection with our seas. If you don't have easy access to the coast, even a day out to the local aquarium can spark the fascination for life in the deep blue. Curiosity feeds young minds, and our ocean has plenty of weird and curious discoveries just waiting to be made.

More Than a Drop in the Ocean

Simple swaps and small actions, when added up, can create a wave of change. Understandably, It can be overwhelming to consider the colossal impact humanity is having on our global ocean. When you stop to take a moment to look around you and see evidence of our influence in real time, it can bring home the seemingly irreparable damage we have done, and are doing. As a result, cases of eco-anxiety – the fear of ecological disaster based upon the planet's current trajectory – are rising, especially among young people. But we mustn't lose hope – ocean optimism is alive and well. You don't have to be an ocean whizz to make a difference. Our collective actions add up. We can all play our part in doing something for the ocean, and our ocean can heal from our past mistakes if given the opportunity to do so. Something is better than nothing, so no matter where you are on your journey to becoming an ocean warrior, you will be making a difference.

6

Discover Your Coastline

The cruel truth of what's happening to our oceans around the world comes with glimmers of optimism. There is a way to turn the tide on the terrible mistakes of humanity's past, but we must act now before it is too late. Now comes the fun bit: discovering our impressive coastline for yourself and getting stuck into our marine world.

Our island nation is ornamented with breathtaking coastal views, and hundreds of adventures await those exploring nature's wonders. Across the UK, Wildlife Trusts sites show off the best that our seas have to offer, and by visiting these sites or becoming a Wildlife Trust member, you can support the incredible work they are doing to help our living seas. Take a look at the map on page 147 and identify your nearest site to explore the coastline, or perhaps make plans for your next staycation.

As enchanting as our coastline is, it can also be a dangerous place, and lives are easily lost at sea. For this reason, whether you're going fossil hunting, splashing in the sea, or participating in a beach clean, it's vital that you check tide times and stay away from loose rocks and cliff edges. Rocks are particularly slippery when wet, so be careful when traversing them, and watch out for sharp edges too. Keeping your wellbeing in mind is especially important if you're going to a remote beach on your own or with a small group of people. Nobody wants what should be a glorious day exploring the seaside to take a turn for the worst. Safety must always come first. In the UK we are blessed to have the Royal National Lifeboat

Institution (RNLI), which provides lifeboat search and rescue, lifeguards and water safety education. It is largely made up of volunteers and supported by public donations. The RNLI website features a considerable amount of

information for safety at sea and the best telephone numbers to contact if the unfortunate should happen.

Always wear ocean-friendly sunscreen on a trip to the beach, even on those overcast days. Make sure you pack plenty of water and some snacks too as many of the most picturesque coastal spots are also the most remote, making it difficult to buy water and other products whilst on the move. Follow the Wildlife Trusts' Seashore Code, which is available online, to make sure you're leaving the coast in a better condition than when you found it. However you choose to experience our shores, make sure you do it responsibly. But most of all, enjoy your time at the seaside. Splash about in the surf, explore the shoreline in search of shells, and breathe in the fresh salty sea air to relax your mind. The sky is the limit when it comes to seaside activities you can enjoy, so whatever floats your boat you can have a fantastic time on our coasts.

Sun, Sea, Sand and Sport

Fresh air and exercise are the perfect combination to improve our mental and physical health, and there are many water-based and land-based sports and activities that you can do along our coastline. Whether you windsurf or kayak, play catch with your dog or simply go for a walk, time spent by the sea can improve your overall wellbeing. The best part is that there are activities for every age and every level of physical activity, so no matter what you choose you can get your salty fix.

Take a Walk

Sand and shingle are much harder to walk or run on than traditional surfaces like tarmac or grass. For this reason, you can burn up to 50 percent more calories by going for a walk or run along the beach. It's a great all-round workout too, as you are improving not only your cardiovascular health, but also your musculature by conditioning your muscles. Walking or running on a sandy beach can also be gentler on your joints.

Beach Yoga

Why not grab your yoga mat and head to the beach first thing in the morning?

With the soothing sound of waves lapping against the shore, the smell of a salty breeze and the feeling of sand between your toes, yoga at the beach is a great way to start the day. The sensory experience of being beside the sea can deepen your relaxation, whilst the challenge of holding poses on a new surface can add a new dimension to your yoga practice. Beach yoga classes are growing in popularity, so there may be a session you can join when you are next at a beach if you don't want to give it a go alone.

Get Fishing

Sea angling is a fantastic way to relax and unwind. Science has shown that it can do wonders for your mental and physical health, and can also be a gateway for connecting people with the natural world. Spending time by the water is linked with lower stress, and angling is even being trialled as a therapy for certain mental health conditions and veteran rehabilitation. Make sure you're always adhering to best-practice handling guidelines and recycle your fishing line using the Anglers National Line Recycling Scheme, so it doesn't entangle marine life. For more information join the Angling Trust and take part in their Get Fishing campaign to learn all you need to know about fishing safely.

Go Paddling

If you don't want to commit to plunging your whole body into the water, why not try feeling

need to keep you warm. If you're taking part in cold-water swimming it's a good idea to do it gradually, and with a wetsuit initially, as the freezing temperatures can cause a shock to your system. It's recommended that you join a cold-water or wild-swimming group.

All Aboard!

Your brain on a boat is a marvellous thing. Feeling the sunshine on your skin, no matter how weak or strong, and being surrounded by water and fresh air can do wonders for your health. If you don't like swimming, heading out on a boat trip can also be a great way of venturing out to sea to explore our coastline without getting wet.

the surf wash over your feet and legs instead? The sensation of sand drifting between your toes and the gentle pull of the surf rolling over your feet can be therapeutic. If the water is clear enough, paddling provides a great opportunity for peering into the underwater world from above the waves. Perhaps you may spot a tiny fish, or a hermit crab scuttling along the strandline.

Swim in the Sea

What's more refreshing that swimming in the sea? Seawater is rich in magnesium. This wonder element is linked with promoting deeper sleep, stimulating rest and repair and triggering the release of the feel-good hormones dopamine and serotonin. Cold-water swimming in particular is highly beneficial for your overall health and wellbeing as it improves your circulation in response to the

Go Diving

Scuba diving is a popular pastime in the UK. You will need specialist equipment for diving, and in the chilly waters surrounding our coast it's also necessary to wear a drysuit to keep warm. Taking your first breath underwater is a unique experience, and in order to do so you'll need to become a qualified diver with a registered organisation such as BSAC. If you don't fancy taking the plunge, why not grab a snorkel or try a freediving course instead? You don't need to invest in expensive attire to explore the underwater world during the summer months.

Surf's Up!

Surfing is a great cardiovascular exercise. The workout you get through surfing builds up heart strength through a mixture of paddling and balancing on the board. As with other water-based activities, by learning to surf you can join a community of like-minded people and make a new community of friends with whom to enjoy the ocean. It's not for the faint-hearted though, as it takes a lot of practice and falling into crashing waves whilst you're learning.

Mini Adventurers

For children, the coast presents an infinite number of opportunities to unleash their inner explorer. Investigating the strandline to see what's been washed up, searching for shells or making a sand castle are all fantastic ways to spend a day at the beach. The coast also offers plenty of inspiration for budding geologists, biologists and photographers.

Hunt for Fossils

England's south-west coastline is a hotspot for fossils, with the Jurassic Coast in Dorset being a world-famous destination for ammonites. Make sure you know the Fossil Code (available on the UK Fossils website) when finding your prehistoric treasures and don't forget to maintain awareness of your surroundings too.

Seaside Safari

The Wildlife Trusts have developed a collection of nifty wildlife spotter guides available to download from their website, which will assist with your own seaside safari. Make the most of your next trip to the seaside by clambering

over rocks, navigating the surf, and maybe even dunking your head underwater in search of marine critters to tick off your checklist. What's high on your UK bucket list to spot?

Explore the Wonders of a Rockpool

Rockpooling is best at low tide, as this is when the rockpools are left exposed by the saltwater and it's easier to identify the sea life within them. Sea anemones, hermit

crabs and small fish like gobies are common sights within rockpools along our coastline. You will probably find many species of seaweed and bivalves such as mussels. Low tide will allow you to navigate the slippier rocks as carefully as possible. It's always best to wear shoes when rockpooling to provide you with more grip whilst exploring the rocky edges. Don't forget to keep an eye on the time and tide! When the water starts raising again, it's time to head up shore.

Grab Your Camera

There's always something to photograph along the seashore. Whether you have a phone camera or the latest digital equipment, you can take fantastic photos of marine life. Get creative and visit the coast at different times of day to play with the lighting – dawn and dusk usually provide attractive light for photography. Wildlife sightings also vary depending on the time of year, so check out the Wildlife Trusts website for what you can see near you.

Beachcombing

As you wander along the seashore, why don't you keep an eye out for the washed-up treasures you may find? Driftwood, shark eggcases and shells are common sights across the shoreline in the UK. Remember that it's against the law to take any natural materials like sand and pebbles from UK beaches, so make sure you leave everything behind – unless it's non-natural material like plastic waste that may have been carried by the tide.

Become a Citizen Scientist

Science is the way in which we learn more about the world around us. It's how we make new discoveries and learn about our relationship with the natural world. There is always new information to discover and investigate. The world is wide and our influence upon is extensive, so it is difficult for scientists to gather all the data they need to make accurate assessments of our impact and decide the best course of action to take. That's where you can help. Citizen science projects are becoming increasingly popular as a way of engaging the public with key environmental issues, connecting them with the natural world and filling important gaps in our scientific knowledge. There are a variety of projects to

get your teeth into depending on your interests and your access to the coast, so why not try one out?

Shoresearch

Shoresearch is the Wildlife Trusts' national citizen science survey of the intertidal shore. By joining their programme, you can learn to identify shoreline seaweed and wildlife species, and help conservationists monitor this habitat. The data collected through this project is used to inform the management of the intertidal region – where land meets sea – and to

WHAT IS CITIZEN SCIENCE?

Collecting data is central to conservation work. It's tough for scientists, conservationists and policymakers to protect species if they don't know much about them. By gathering information on a species and its population, such as its distribution behaviour and feeding habitats, we can learn how best to protect it. Monitoring populations is also vital so we can understand how human behaviour influences species and identify issues and potential solutions before they become a significant problem. In many cases, the data available is insufficient to reach a successful conclusion. That's where citizen science can help. These projects rely on members of the public and trained volunteers who submit relevant data to plug the gaps in our understanding of the studied species or ecosystem. Often all that's required is an enthusiasm for the environment and an interest in learning on the job, with dedicated training or identification guides usually provided to help you along your way. Citizen science projects are an excellent way for you to dive into your local marine environment and make a big difference in its conservation locally, nationally and even internationally.

monitor the effects of pollution, climate change and invasive species on fragile marine species. Shoresearch data has even been used to help designate Marine Conservation Zones in England.

Join the Big Seaweed Search

Seaweed distributions are changing. Since 2009, citizen scientists have been contributing data on the 650 species of seaweed found on our shores through the Big Seaweed Search. Seaweed creates habitats where fish, invertebrates, birds and marine mammals find food and shelter. Observations give us a better picture of how seaweeds are affected by rising sea temperature, the arrival and spread of non-native species, and ocean acidification. The project is run in collaboration with the Natural History Museum and the Marine Conservation Society. Information on how to get involved is available on the Big Seaweed Search website.

Be a Seagrass Spotter

SeagrassSpotter is a collaborative project between Project Seagrass and the universities of Cardiff and Swansea. This global project allows citizen scientists to contribute to marine conservation through an app on their phones and share their observations with an enormous network of scientists. Whether you're a keen angler, scuba diver or a visitor to the coast, you can take part in this internationally important project. With your help, through SeagrassSpotter, researchers hope to implement more seagrass restoration projects around the world and to learn more about this fragile and vitally important ocean habitat.

Report a Stranding

While the UK coastline is one of the best in Europe for spotting whales, dolphins,

porpoises and seals, unfortunately there are terribly sad occasions when these animals become stranded on our shores. In certain circumstances, they are unable to refloat themselves or are too weak to make the journey back out to sea and so they perish. The Cetacean Strandings Investigation Partnership (CSIP) are responsible for investigating any stranding events of whales and dolphins that take place on our shores, and occasionally also examine other rarer species, like basking sharks. You can contact them via the Natural History Museum website. If you'd like to go further, it is also possible for you to become trained as British Divers Marine Life Medic and assist with stranding events and rescue attempts of marine life.

Great Eggcase Hunt

Mermaid's purses (top right), the discarded eggcases of all skates and egg-laying sharks, are often encountered during a walk to the beach. By reporting your sightings you can help the Shark Trust to better understand the health of shark and skate populations here in the UK.

They have developed a handy guide, which is available to download from their website to identify which species the eggcase came from. Eggcases wash up all year round, so whatever the time of year keep your eyes peeled and make sure you register your sightings online.

National Whale and Dolphin Watch

Hosted by the Sea Watch Foundation, this annual weekly event, during which members of the public submit their sightings, provides a general snapshot of what is in UK coastal waters over a short period. There is a general lack of awareness of the great diversity of whales, dolphins and porpoises in our seas, despite them being commonly encountered, and the event helps to plug this gap. You can also sign up to be trained by the ORCA Foundation to be a marine mammal observer and to join trips across the Bay of Biscay to record observed cetacean numbers passing through the area.

Where to Visit: Dive into Nature

You may now be wondering where the best places are to experience the diverse array of species residing within the UK's coastal and marine environments in person. The Wildlife Trusts' reserves are a great place to start. They have a fantastic collection of sites across the UK, many of which run hands-on discovery days, where you can experience the wonders of life below the waves yourself. To get you started on your UK coastal adventure, the map below and next few pages reveal just some of the best Wildlife Trusts sites available for you to explore.

North Sea

Handa Island ●

N

Atlantic Ocean

Shetland Islands

Orkney Islands

Seaton Cliffs ●

Cresswell Foreshore ●

North Sea

Isle of Muck ●

Ayres Nature Discovery Centre ● and Nature Trail

● Hunt Cliff

● South Walney

Spurn National Nature Reserve

The Ribble Estuary ●

Donna Nook National Nature Reserve

Irish Sea

Holme Dunes ●

● Morfa Bychan

Colne Point Nature Reserve

Sedger's Bank ●

Milton Locks Nature Reserve

Atlantic Ocean

The Fine Foundation Wild Seas Centre ●

● Seaford Head

English Channel

0   100   200km
scale

West Coast and ● Burhou Islands Ramsar Site

Cresswell Foreshore

rockpools filled with life like the shanny, butterfish and porcelain crab, are uncovered by the receding water. Marine flora at this site is also noteworthy, with a variety of seaweeds like the delicate feathery coral weed being found here.

Cresswell Foreshore, Northumberland Wildlife Trust

A fascinating site for its geology, Cresswell Foreshore is a large wave-cut platform with numerous shallow rockpools enticing diverse marine life and wading birds including turnstone, purple sandpiper, sanderling and ringed plover. Cresswell Foreshore is the ideal location to explore rolling sand dunes for as far as the eye can see. When the tide is low,

Hunt Cliff, Tees Valley Wildlife Trust

The dramatic headlands of Hunt Cliff, one of the highest cliffs on the east English coast, make it the perfect location for seabirds to soar high in the sky and nest along the perilous cliff edge. Colonies of kittiwakes can be heard and smelt long before they are spotted, from their arrival in February until their departure in August. Kittiwakes can be distinguished from other gulls by their 'ink-dipped' black wing-tips. The cliff face is of regional importance for nesting kittiwakes and other seabirds such as fulmars and cormorants. You can watch seabirds from the beach at Saltburn, or from the cliff top as they soar on thermals, returning to their nests with food for their young.

Spurn National Nature Reserve, Yorkshire Wildlife Trust

Celebrated by birdwatchers for its autumn migration spectacle, Spurn National Nature Reserve can be a brilliantly wild place over the winter months. The peninsula is secluded from the mainland at high tide, so it is imperative to check the tide schedule carefully before venturing out on the 3.5-mile route to the point. On the estuary site of Spurn, you will observe knot feeding on the Humber mudflats alongside other wading birds. On the seaward side look out for harbour porpoises and grey seals as they take refuge close to the coast.

Hunt Cliff

Spurn National Nature Reserve

Donna Nook National Nature Reserve, Lincolnshire Wildlife Trust

Famed for its breeding colony of grey seals, Donna Nook should be high on your must-see coastal list. Over 2,000 seal pups are born here every winter, providing a heart-warming chance to observe these adorable animals from a viewing area close to the colony. By sticking to the designated area visitors, you ensure their safety and lower the risk of disturbing resting seals. Donna Nook is comprised of dunes and intertidal areas. As a result of coastal processes, the natural features of the site are continually changing, so there's always something new to see.

Holme Dunes, Norfolk Wildlife Trust

Holme Dunes in the far north-west corner of Norfolk offers keen birdwatchers opportunities to encounter migrating birds like oystercatchers, curlews and redshanks. Beyond the area where the Wash meets the North Sea, this location features an array of coastal habitats, which provide shelter for some of the

Donna Nook National Nature Reserve

Holme Dunes

UK's rarest wildlife, including natterjack toads. Plant life here is notable too. Sea buckthorn, for example, is a spiky silvery shrub that is prevalent here, and helps stabilise the dunes. In autumn, its bright orange berries are a blessing to the thousands of migrating birds, such as wintering thrushes, that stop off at Holme.

Colne Point Nature Reserve, Essex Wildlife Trust

Located along the mouth of the Colne Estuary, Colne Point is an intricate expanse of saltmarsh and creek habitats formed by Ray Creek, which meanders through the vast saltmarsh before greeting the shingle-lined beach that hugs the shore. The mudflats provide rich feeding grounds, attracting an impressive array of migratory wading birds. Colne Point holds a number of designations of international and national significance, including being a RAMSAR wetland site, a Special Protection Area and a National Nature Reserve. The nationally rare golden samphire and small cord-grass are also found here.

Seaford Head, Sussex Wildlife Trust

Dramatic coastal seascapes are on offer at Seaford Head in Sussex. A panoramic view of the awe-inspiring Seven Sisters cliffs and

Seaford Head

Colne Point Nature Reserve

Cuckmere Valley can be enjoyed, providing the perfect escape from the rush of everyday life. These rolling chalk cliffs are not the only offering though. Seaford Head falls within the Beachy Head West Marine Conservation Zone and is a Site of Special Scientific Interest.

Milton Locks Nature Reserve, Hampshire and Isle of Wight Wildlife Trust

For those looking for a natural hideaway close to Portsmouth, Milton Locks Nature Reserve on Portsea Island is just the ticket. Only 1 hectare in size, this environmental oasis is small but mighty, and jam-packed with diverse habitats. Take a look at saltmarsh specialists like sea aster and purslane, and don't forget to see if you can spot crabs scurrying across the mudflats. When the tide is right you can also peer into the water from the beach to see shoals of tiny fish moving together.

West Coast and Burhou Islands Ramsar Site, Alderney Wildlife Trust

Located within the northern Channel Islands, the West Coast and Burhou Islands are a designated Ramsar site (a wetland site given special designation by UNESCO) for their internationally important seabird populations. Their shallow waters and associated islets are situated within one of the most dynamic tidal systems within UK waters, making them biologically abundant. More than 100 species of seaweed have been recorded here. It's estimated that over 1 percent of the world's gannet population is found on the islets of Ortac and Les Etacs, and the site is also home to an important grey seal colony on Burhou Island.

The Fine Foundation Wild Seas Centre, Dorset Wildlife Trust

Explore the living seas of Dorset's iconic Jurassic Coast by visiting the Fine Foundation Wild Seas Centre in Kimmeridge. The Centre even provides an opportunity for you to get wet and dive into the ocean, by offering an underwater nature trail for snorkellers – perfect for newbies and experienced snorkellers alike. Once under the waves you're likely to encounter a stunning diversity of fish. Connemara clingfish and Montagu's blennies can be found hiding between the rocky crevices, and colourful wrasse can be spotted swimming

West Coast and Burhou Islands Ramsar Site

The Fine Foundation Wild Seas Centre

among the rainbow wrack. If you're lucky, you could come across marine mammals like seals and dolphins, but be sure to give them plenty of space.

The Ribble Estuary, Lancashire Wildlife Trust

The Ribble Estuary is one of the most significant sites in the UK for wintering wildfowl. It supports more than 250,000 ducks, geese, swans and waders, and is internationally important for 16 species of wintering birds. Many are enticed by the smelt and eel that make the most of its muddy areas. Arrivals begin from September: wigeon from eastern Russia; whooper swans and pink-footed geese from Iceland; and Bewick's swans from Siberia. Black-tailed godwits have bred on Newton Marsh, on The Fylde, since 1988. The Ribble Estuary National Nature Reserve covers over half of the Ribble estuary and is managed by Natural England.

Ayres Nature Discovery Centre and Nature Trail, Isle of Man Wildlife Trust

An 8km expanse of precious sand dunes,

The Ribble Estuary

South Walney, Cumbria Wildlife Trust

With sweeping views across the sprawling Morecambe Bay, South Walney delivers a unique insight into the wild Cumbrian coast. It is a sanctuary for seabirds year-round, and provides some of the best birdwatching in the country. You can spot mixed herring and lesser black-backed gull colonies here, as well as an assembly of wading birds during the winter months. South Walney is also home to the only grey seal colony in Cumbria, making it a must-see for all wildlife enthusiasts.

stretching from Cronk-y-Bing to the Point of Ayre, makes the Ayre Nature Discovery Centre the perfect location to explore. It's also an ecologically important site with a range of designations, including Area of Special Scientific Interest (ASSI) and a National Nature Reserve (NNR). Head out along the nature trail and meander through the marram dunes from the shingle beach onto a diverse expanse of heathland. Alongside outstanding scenery, there are plenty of species to spot, including diving northern gannets and sand lizards (above) in the dunes.

Handa Island, Scottish Wildlife Trust

Towering above the crashing waves, Handa Island is a magnet for seabirds off the west coast of Scotland. It is an internationally important breeding site for many spectacular seabirds: guillemots, razorbills and great skuas that spend the summer months breeding and feeding around the island. The island's rich

South Walney

Handa Island

Seaton Cliffs

of Arbroath, on the east coast of Scotland, approximately 15 miles from Dundee. These remarkable red sandstone cliffs are home to a myriad of habitats that support an abundance of biodiversity. The Angus Coastal Route, linking the cities of Dundee and Aberdeen, passes through the reserve providing the perfect tranquil escape from busy city life. You can spot bottlenose dolphins as you cast your eye out to the sea year-round. May to July delivers optimum seabird watching conditions when you can spot Arctic and common terns returning from foraging at sea – and perhaps even an arctic skua, too, if you're lucky.

Isle of Muck, Ulster Wildlife Trust

Home to the third-largest colony of cliff-nesting seabirds in Northern Ireland, the Isle of Muck should be on every seabird enthusiast's must-see list. Fulmar, shag, kittiwake and razorbill are just a handful of the species that nest on the island every summer. The surrounding ocean is buzzing with life and is one of the best places in Northern Ireland to see cetaceans like harbour porpoises and both common and grey seals. There is no public access to the island to ensure the breeding seabirds aren't disturbed. Still, thankfully you can observe these soaring seabirds from afar along the mainland's shores.

waters support tens of thousands of seabirds that migrate here every spring. Rising from the ocean, these incredible cliffs offer panoramic sea views to grab a pair of binoculars and spot iconic marine mammals like minke whales, Risso's dolphins, grey seals and perhaps even a rare orca.

Seaton Cliffs, Scottish Wildlife Trust

Fiery red sea caves, arches and stacks decorate the coast alongside the seaside town

Isle of Muck

Sedger's Bank, South and West Wales Wildlife Trust

Sedger's Bank is a coastal gem on the rugged coast of Port Eynon Bay. Its rocky shoreline is alive with a wealth of marine wildlife like beadlet anemones clinging to tidal pools and purple sandpipers foraging along the strandline. Most of the reserve is typically covered by seawater and can only be viewed in its entirety during the lowest tides of the year.

An oarweed kelp forest decorates the reserve's perimeter and is a great place to explore underwater during high tides. Grey seals can also be seen here hauling out along the reserve's banks.

Morfa Bychan, North Wales Wildlife Trust

With coastal developments putting heightened pressure on fragile dune environments, Morfa Bychan offers a rare opportunity for visitors to explore these precious ecosystems. The undulating dunes accompanied by the soothing sound of crashing waves make this an ideal spot for a summer getaway. Maybe you'll even spot a harbour porpoise playing in the surf!

Embarking on Your Coastal Discovery

Across the UK, there are plenty of wildlife sites and dramatic coastal landscapes to suit your needs. We can also get hands-on with conservation, now that citizen science projects are rising in popularity and number. Through projects like those, you can see with your own eyes the marine marvels that we have highlighted throughout this book, humanity's impact on our coast, and our attempts to rectify past mistakes. As you discover your favourite coastal Wildlife Trust site, you will uncover a living coastline that will hopefully capture your imagination in a way no other environment can. Whether you choose to meander along the coast with friends and family on a chilly winter morning, grab a pair of binoculars to observe seabirds soaring through the sky or whales breaching offshore, or you just lay down a towel on the sand to soak in the sunshine and listen to the waves crashing against the shoreline, there are so many ways you can enjoy our coastlines. The very dynamism that makes them so abundant with life can equally provide you with an infinite number of discoveries and experiences on every trip. You can be a responsible citizen too by picking up a few pieces of litter on each trip as a little thank you to the big blue. Maybe you will even choose to inspire others by sharing your coastal adventures online through a blog or posting your photos. From the wild and rugged coast of the Shetland Islands to the sun-soaked beaches of Cornwall, there are so many natural marine wonders for you to encounter – so what are you waiting for? Time to get out there.

Sedger's Bank

Morfa Bychan

The Future is Blue

When it comes to our seas, and the intricacies of their conservation, there is a lot to take in. Whether you feel inspired, angry or overwhelmed, you can channel your feelings into creating a sustainable future for our global ocean. Feel empowered to take action and experience the majesty of the ocean.

Whatever your motivation, you can now use it to join the tsunami of change that is needed to protect our seas. Without the ocean, our world as we know it would cease to exist. Its ability to supply oxygen, regulate the climate and deliver food security is quickly waning as a result of our poor decisions. Our ocean provides life on our planet with the means to thrive, but we need to manage it sustainably for it to continue to do so. We need to do our bit for the ocean so it can do its job for us.

The future of our blue world is in our hands. What we decide to do in the next ten years will define the coming decades. On the international stage, we are seeing growing support for ocean recovery – but is it enough? The clock is ticking. People from every walk of life are uniting to join the conversation and take action for our living seas. The fight for a healthy ocean will be a long and arduous one. We must continue to push through the challenges to reach the ultimate goal of sustainable seas for us all. There still isn't an equal seat at the table for every member of our global community during this conversation, but our collective success depends on there being one. Raising our voices for our ocean sometimes means sitting back and listening in order to give space to those from under-represented groups, such as indigenous communities, ethnic minorities and women, to have their voices heard. To achieve sustainable seas in the western world, we need to unravel decades of culture that focused on maximising profits, regardless of the exploitative costs. We need to start seeing the ocean as an ally rather than an unlimited resource to fill our bellies and line our wallets.

But you don't have to be a marine scientist, a politician, or an environmental campaigner to make a difference for our seas. There is power in numbers, and now is your time to shine. Share your love for the ocean far and wide. Immerse yourself in the bountiful blue; feel its cool salty water slipping in between your toes; breathe in the fresh sea air and the other unique smells of a bustling coastline; listen to the loud yet soothing sounds of the waves crashing against the coast. The ocean touches all our lives, including yours. Your voice matters, and you can use it to protect what you love. We can have a thriving ocean. So get out there, take action and explore the bountiful blue – Britain's living seas are ready and waiting for you.

RESOURCE LIST

- Angling Trust – www.anglingtrust.net
- Anglers National Line Recycling Scheme
- www.anglers-nlrs.co.uk
- Aquaculture Stewardship Council
- www.asc-aqua.org
- Big Seaweed Search – Natural History Museum & Marine Conservation Society
- www.bigseaweedsearch.org
- British Divers Marine Life Rescue – Become a Marine Mammal Medic – www.bdmlr.org.uk/become-a-marine-mammal-medic
- British Sub-Aqua Club
- www.bsac.com/home
- Marine Conservation Society – Good Fish Guide – www.mcsuk.org/goodfishguide
- Marine Stewardship Council
- www.msc.org/uk
- ORCA Foundation – Train to be a Marine Mammal Surveyor
- www.orcaweb.org.uk/get-involved/train-to-be-a-marine-mammal-surveyor
- Project Seagrass – SeagrassSpotter
- www.seagrassspotter.org
- Royal National Lifeboat Institution (RNLI)
- www.rnli.org
- Sea Watch Foundation – National Whale and Dolphin Watch – www.seawatchfoundation.org.uk/nwdw
- Shark Trust | Great Eggcase Hunt
- www.sharktrust.org/great-eggcase-hunt
- UK Cetacean Strandings Investigation Programme (CSIP) | Report a Stranding
- www.ukstrandings.org/how-to-report-a-stranding
- UK Fossils – Fossil Code
- www.ukfossils.co.uk/code-of-conduct
- Wildlife Trusts – Seaside Safari
- www.wildlifetrusts.org/where_to_seaside_holiday
- Wildlife Trusts – Shoresearch
- www.wildlifetrusts.org/get-involved/other-ways-get-involved/shoresearch

ACKNOWLEDGEMENTS

From scientists researching the weird and wonderful to conservationists working tirelessly to protect our ocean, the young people who have passion and drive for sustainable seas to the fishers who depend on its riches, thank you for inspiring an ocean-positive future.

Without my family, friends and colleagues, this book would not have been possible. Thank you for making me laugh, being a shoulder to cry on and for listening to endless recitals of this book in various iterations. Thank you to everyone who provided photographs and told their stories from the frontline of marine conservation. The sea is in our blood, and I am continually in awe of the dedication you all have to life below the waves. A special dedication to my grandmother who sadly did not make it to the end of this journey with us, but her light continues to shine on.

Thank you also to the wonderful people at Bloomsbury who allowed me to share my love for the ocean through this book and their continued patience during a globally tricky time.

Let's not forget you holding this book now, either. Thank you for joining the movement to protect the big blue. It will take an ocean of people to generate the waves of change needed to turn the tide on the future of our seas. The power is in our hands and now is the time to act.

We can all be everyday heroes for our ocean, and this book is dedicated to everyone who stands up for our living seas.

Picture Credits

Bloomsbury Publishing would like to thank the following for providing photographs and for permission to reproduce copyright material in this book. While every effort has been made to trace and acknowledge all copyright holders, we would like to apologise for any errors or omissions and invite readers to inform us so that we can make corrections to future editions.

Key

t = top; l = left; tl = top left; tr = top right; c = centre;
b = bottom; bl = bottom left; bc = bottom centre;
br = bottom right.

Abbreviated photo sources

AL = Alamy; FL = FLPA/Minden Pictures; G = Getty Images; NPL = Nature Picture Library; SS = Shutterstock.

Front cover Alex Mustard/NPL; **back cover** t SS, SS, Alex Mustard/NPL, b Christopher Hopefitch/G; **1** Dan Burton/NPL; **2/3** Alex Mustard/NPL; **4/5** Alex Mustard/NPL; **8/9** Alex Mustard/NPL; **10** SS; **11** Photo Escapes/robertharding/G; **12** t SCOTLAND: The Big Picture/NPL, c SS, b Jeremy Woodhouse/G; **13** t Joanne Hedger/G, b SS; **14** t SS, b SS; **15** t SS, b SS; **16** t stevendocwra/G, b SS; **17** t SS, c Sandra Standbridge/G, b Sandra Standbridge/G; **18** Siobhan Fraser/G; **19** t Sarah Hodgson/Dorset Wildlife Trust, b James Warwick/G; **20** t SS, b SS; **21** t Nick Upton/AL, c Frank Hecker/AL, b SS; **22** t Crown copyright, b Kevin Britland/UIG/G; **23** t Tim E White/G, b Nick Upton/NPL; **24** t Nick Upton/NPL, c Reinhard Dirscherl/G, b Alex Mustard/NPL; **25** t Paul Kay/G, b Alex Mustard/NPL; **26** t J Shepherd/G, c Alex Mustard/NPL, b SS; **27** t Sue Daly/NPL, c Nick Davies/G, b SS, **28** t SCOTLAND: The Big Picture/NPL, b SS; **29** t D.P. Wilson/FL, b Alex Mustard/NPL; **30** t Tim Bow/G, b Alex Mustard/NPL; **31** t blickwinkel/AL, b Sue Daly/NPL; **32** t Alex Mustard/NPL, b Alex Mustard/NPL; **33** t creacart/G, b Sue Daly/NPL; **34** t Sue Daly/NPL, c Sue Daly/NPL, b Anne Coatesy/NPL; **35** t Alex Mustard/2020VISION, c SS, b Linda Pitkin/2020VISION/NPL; **36** t SS, c Doug Perrine/NPL, b Alex Walker/G; **37** t Alex Mustard/NPL, b Richard Herrmann/NPL; **38** t Alex Mustard/NPL, b Wild Wonders of Europe/Carwardine/NPL; **39** t SCOTLAND: The Big Picture/NPL, b SS; **40** t SS, b SS; **41** t NPL/AL, b Michele D'Amico supersky77/G; **42/43** fotoVoyager/G; **46** SS; **47** t David Woodfall/NPL, b thislife pictures/G; **48** t SS, b SS; **51** t SS; **52** b SS; **54** t Ashley Cooper/G, b SS; **56** t Fiona Crouch, b Bryce Stewart; **57** t Gary Yeowell/G, b SS; **58** t David Snow/EyeEm/G, b Dougal Waters/G; **59** t Doug Perrine/NPL, b Sami Sarkis/G; **60/61** Adam Black/EyeEm/G; **62** Tom Kidd/AL; **64** Dodge65/G; **67** t SS, b SS; **68** Alex Mustard/NPL; **69** Science History Images/AL; **70** t SS, b SS; **71** t SS, b SS; **72** t Sergio Hanquet/NPL, c SS, b Sarah Hodgson/

Dorset Wildlife Trust; **73** SS; **74** SS; **75** SCOTLAND: The Big Picture/NPL; **76** David Noton/NPL; **77** tl SS, tr Upix Photography/AL, b SS; **78** Dominic Robinson/AL; **79** SS; **80** t SS, b Wild Wonders of Europe/Geslin/NPL; **81** t SS, b SS; **82** SS; **83** SS; **84** Philippe Clement/NPL; **85** Chris Gomersall/2020VISION/NPL; **86** ton koene/AL; **88** t Gavin Newman/AL, b Ashley Cooper/G; **89** Norbert Wu/NPL; **91** t SS, b Monty Rakusen/G; **92** SS; **93** Peter Cairns/2020VISION/NPL; **94/95** Alex Mustard/NPL; **96** Abstract Aerial Art/G; **97** shomos Uddin/G; **98** Fiona Crouch; **99** Ocean Conservation Trust; **100** t Alex Mustard/2020VISION/NPL, b SS; **101** Matt Uttley, ENORI and Blue Marine Foundation; **102** Joe Burn; **104** SS; **105** t Sue Daly/NPL, b SS; **106** Christopher Hope-Fitch/G; **107** t SS, b Polly Whyte; **108** t Derek Haslam, b SS; **109** t SS, b Francis Jeffcock; **110** t sOulsurfing - Jason Swain/G, b SS; **111** t ajsissues/AL, b SS; **112** t Morgan Trimble/AL, b SS; **114** Monty Rakusen/G; **115** Alex Mustard/NPL; **116/117** SS; **118** SS; **119** SS; **120** t SS, b blue sky in my pocket/G; **121** t Ashley Cooper/G, c Danny Green/NPL, b SS; **122** t SS, b SS; **123** t SS, c SS, b SS; **124** t Fine to Flush/Water UK, b SS; **125** t SS, c SS, b SS; **126** SS; **127** SS; **128** t SS, b SS; **129** t Marine Stewardship Council, b SS; **130** SS; **131** SS; **132** t SS, b SS; **133** David Miller/Celtic Deep; **134** t SS, b Skully/AL; **136/137** MBI/A; **138** t Tony Quinn/EyeEm/G, b SS; **139** t SS, b Dougal Waters/G; **140/141** t Peter Cade/G; **140** b JAG IMAGES/G; **141** c Tim Platt/G, b Peter Cade/G; **142** t Gary Yeowell/G, b lucentius/G; **143** t Johner Images/G, b Christopher Hopefitch/G; **144** t Josh Symes/Cornwall Wildlife Trust Shoresearch; **145** t J Shepherd/G, b British Divers Marine Life Rescue; **146** t SS; b Catherine Clark/ www.cjdolfinphotography.co.uk/G; **148** t Duncan Hutt, b Findlay/AL; **149** t SS, b Marco Reeuwijk/G; **150** t SS, c SS, b SS; **151** t Paul Gonella, b Joshua Copping; **152** t SS, b SS; **153** t Manx Wildlife Trust, bl SS, br SS; **154** t SS, b Robert Thompson/NPL; **155** t SS; b Charles Hawes/G.

The illustrations on pages 7, 49, 50, 52, 53 and 147 are © Bloomsbury Publishing and were commissioned from JB Illustrations for *Britain's Living Seas*.

Index